A GREAT WALL 北京故事

A Learning Guide

To Accompany the Peter Wang film *A Great Wall*
Screenplay by Peter Wang and Shirley Sun

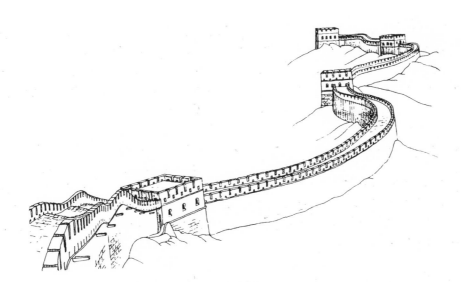

Jing-heng Ma

馬靜桓編

Second Edition

Published by
Center for Chinese Studies, The University of Michigan
104 Lane Hall, Ann Arbor MI 48109-1290, U.S.A.

Second Edition

First Printing 1990
Second Printing 1993
Third Printing 1997

Story content and dialogue of the film *A Great Wall*
written by Peter Wang and Shirley Sun.
Copyright © 1985 by W & S Productions.
Film dialogue transcribed by permission of W & S Productions
(594 Broadway, Suite 906, New York NY 10012);
to be used for teaching purposes only.

Printed and made in the United States of America

⊗ The paper used in this publication meets the requirements
of the American National Standard for Information Sciences—
Permanence of Paper for Publications and Documents
in Libraries and Archives ANSI/NISO/Z39.48—1992.

ISBN 978-0-89264-112-3 (alk. paper) (pbk.)
ISBN 0-89264-112-6 (alk. paper) (pbk.)

Contents

Acknowledgments

I would like to acknowledge a number of people who have assisted me in the preparation of this study guide. First and foremost, I would like to express my deepest appreciation to Peter Wang and Shirley Sun for allowing me to use their film as the basis for this teaching text. I would also like to thank Peter Wang for the hours he spent editing the manuscript.

Very special thanks are extended to Karen Hubbard, who contributed many of the ideas used in formatting this text. I greatly appreciate the time and effort she spent in transcribing the English text from the film and typing the English portions of the manuscript.

I wish to express my sincere thanks to my colleague Theresa Yao and her third-year students of Chinese for testing this material at Wellesley College in the fall of 1989. Their enthusiasm for the material was a constant source of encouragement. Their suggestions and ideas were also invaluable in the prepartion of the final manuscript. I am grateful as well to my other colleagues at Wellesley College, Ruby Lam and Jia Ni, for the time and effort they spent reading this manuscript. Their comments and criticisms were much appreciated.

I owe a special debt of gratitude to the reviewers of this manuscript, Professors Shuen-fu Lin and William Baxter, both at The University of Michigan, for their insightful comments and suggestions. I would also like to acknowledge The University of Michigan Center for Chinese Studies for its continuing interest in publishing this teaching material for students of Chinese. Special thanks are extended to JoAnne Lehman and Walter Michener for their editorial skills and guidance.

Finally, I would like to thank my husband for his continued support and encouragement.

Jing-heng Ma
January 1990

This second edition includes a complete *pinyin* transcription of the script, prepared by Galal Walker and his assistants in the Department of East Asian Languages and Literatures at The Ohio State University. To them also, my thanks.

August 1993

Preface

A Great Wall: A Learning Guide is a textbook for intermediate-level study of the Chinese language. It is designed for use with the video film **A Great Wall** 北京故事, which was written by Peter Wang 王正方 and Shirley Sun 孙小铃 , directed by Peter Wang, and produced by W & S Productions.* The film's setting, dialogue, and theme make it an invaluable tool for teaching Western students about the language and culture of China.

I developed this text during the summer of 1989 in collaboration with Karen Hubbard, a graduate student of the Center for Chinese Studies at The University of Michigan. Ms. Hubbard and I trust that our joint effort, which has involved many rounds of experimentation and revision, has resulted in an enjoyable and effective course of study.

This learning guide is prepared especially for students at an intermediate level. Prerequisite to its use is proficiency in the basics of Chinese grammar and vocabulary as presented in textbooks such as Parker Po-fei Huang and Hugh M. Stimson's **Spoken Standard Chinese I & II** and **Written Standard Chinese I & II**, J. DeFrancis's **Beginning Chinese** and **Beginning Chinese Reader Parts I & II**, or Henry C. Fenn and M. Gardner Tewksbury's **Speak Mandarin** and **Read Chinese Books I & II**. The material is presented in both traditional and simplified characters.

The text has been divided into ten sections for convenient study, with each section containing a portion of the script, a list of new vocabulary words for each scene in that section, sample sentences for the vocabulary, and exercises. At the beginning of each section, cues have been added to call students' attention to a few significant details in the film and to prompt further analysis. The script is a direct transcription of the film's dialogue, excluding some background conversation,

---

*   Audiocassettes of the dialogue, recorded by Jing-heng Ma and Wei-yi Ma, and of the vocabulary with sample sentences, recorded by Jing-heng Ma, are available from the publisher of this text: Center for Chinese Studies Publications, 104 Lane Hall, University of Michigan, Ann Arbor, MI 48109 (313/998-7181).

which we encourage the students to decipher for themselves. English dialogue in the script has been included to clarify the tone of conversation and add continuity.

Each section also includes five types of exercises to encourage proper and frequent usage of new words and structures. (All of the exercises are intended for discussion and practice only after viewing the film.) First, questions are provided for *class discussion in Chinese* 課堂討論 . These questions should be answered orally and at length by the students during class time. More complex explanations of aspects of Chinese culture may be prepared by the instructor or researched by the students. Second, ten *questions* 問題 about the film are asked in Chinese, to be answered as thoroughly as possible in writing, using both the new vocabulary and previously learned characters. These and the other written exercises are to be completed by the students at home after they have studied the vocabulary. Third, the students are asked to *create sentences* 造句 that demonstrate the proper usage and context of the new vocabulary. Fourth, English sentences from the script have been selected for *translation* 翻譯 into Chinese. This exercise will challenge students to convert sentence structure, consider word choice, and use interjections and will train them to think before writing. Finally, there is an *essay question* 自由發揮 , which is meant to encourage creativity, analysis, and criticism of the plot and those themes of the film that interest the students.

The vocabulary list consists of 423 items, 62 of which may be considered optional and are marked with asterisks. Many of the optional words are unique to the Beijing dialect and are included to give students exposure to colloquialisms. The students should be able to recall the remaining 361 items from memory and be able to write them correctly. Approximately 45 new words are introduced in each unit. In order to assist teachers, a table listing the number of vocabulary words in each section and scene is provided. As a further resource for students, the 423 vocabulary words are also phonetically indexed, according to the *pinyin* system, at the back of the volume. The index indicates the scene in which each entry occurred and its vocabulary number, and can be used for review and self-testing.

The learning process using this material should begin with visual experience, which should be followed by aural exposure and oral practice. Reading comprehension and written expression should then be used to clarify and reinforce the material to be learned, while guiding the students back into the visual experience. The goal of the process is for students to develop cultural insight along with total competence in communication.

Each instructor's primary concern, of course, will be to meet the needs and goals of his or her particular students. Some suggestions are given here to assist instructors in developing their own methods and schedules for using **A Great Wall**. (In any case, instructors will require audiovisual equipment for frequent in-class use, and copies of both the video and the script cassette should be made available for convenient use in class and in the language lab.)

Before class:

1. First, the students should watch the section of the film that will be discussed in class.
2. Next the students should listen to the same scenes on the dialogue cassette.

In class:

3. Explain the background of the movie and any aspects of Chinese culture that may be of interest.
4. While showing the movie, stop it often (with a remote control) to discuss the scenes. Use as much Chinese as possible, translating only the parts that are the most difficult for the students.
5. Read the script with the students during class and go over the sample sentences that use the new vocabulary.
6. Assign the sentences and written exercises as homework.
7. Review the scenes covered the previous day and continue discussion practice.
8. Ask the students to perform the script, or parts of it, in pairs or small groups. This exercise will help them retain material through memorization, review, and fluid dialogue. Role playing can also be used to test the oral skills of the students periodically and to encourage group study.
9. Give frequent oral and written quizzes and tests.

The *pīnyīn* system of romanization is used in this text for vocabulary pronunciation. This system of romanization was adopted by the People's Republic of China after 1949. Unless otherwise specified, the joining of syllables complies with the practices followed in other literature that uses the *pīnyīn* system. If "n" occurs before a vowel in the middle of a word, it is read as part of the following syllable. For example:

$$\text{yìnián} = \text{yì} + \text{nián}$$

If "ng" appears before a vowel in the middle of a word, "n" is read as part of the preceding syllable and "g" is read as part of the following syllable. For example:

$$\text{zhēnguài} = \text{zhēn} + \text{guài}$$

Exceptions to these rules are marked with an apostrophe. For example:

$$\text{liànai} = \text{liàn'ai}$$
$$\text{Chángān} = \text{Cháng'ān}$$

For standardized sayings, proverbs, idioms, or cliches, hyphens are used to join two or more syllables. For example:

$$\text{rén-shì-tiě, fàn-shì-gāng}$$
$$\text{gǔ-jín-zhōng-wài}$$

Blank spaces indicate syllables which may, under certain conditions, be separated by a pause or by insertion of additional elements. For example:

$$\text{xià lìng}$$
$$\text{qi chē}$$

There are two other film-based learning guides in this series—**Strange Friends** 陌生的朋友 and **At Middle Age** 人到中年 . **Strange Friends** is an intermediate-level text that introduces common conversational Chinese through a film about strangers on a train encountering modern societal dilemmas in China. **Strange Friends** may be used in an intermediate or second-year class prior to use of **A Great Wall**. **At Middle Age**, a more advanced text, is recommended for use in the third year of Chinese language study. The dialogue of **At Middle Age** is a more educated Chinese; the theme of its story is the impact of the Cultural Revolution.

Language learning material of this type is experimental. We welcome suggestions concerning format, content, or corrections for future editions of this text.

Synopsis

The film **A Great Wall** explores the dynamics within and between two families, one Chinese and the other Chinese-American. The film follows the families for a period of about one month, during which the Americans visit their relatives' home in Beijing. While the plot is simple and the tone lighthearted, this is a drama of cultural contrasts that also addresses such themes as racism and class differences.

The story opens on the daily lives of the two families. In San Francisco, Leo Fang, a talented computer engineer, is experiencing problems at work: he is passed over for an anticipated promotion, apparently because of racism. Following a quarrel with his boss, Leo decides to return to China for a visit, along with his family. For his wife, Grace, and their teenaged son, Paul, who have never been to China and do not speak Chinese, the trip is merely an adventure. For Leo, the journey means a reunion with his sister and a return to his childhood roots.

Meanwhile, in Beijing, Lili Zhao and her friend Jan spend their days preparing for the college entrance examination. The girls gradually become friends with two of their male classmates and begin to experiment with romance. Lili's mother, whose husband is a retired official, receives a letter from her brother Leo, announcing the Fang family's visit.

With the Fangs' arrival in Beijing, the two plots merge and cultural contrasts sharpen. As she entertains Paul, her energetic American cousin, Lili is distracted from both her studies and her new boyfriend, Yida. Yida struggles to hold her attention without disappointing his father, who holds ambitions for the boy's future as a scholar and wants him to spend more time studying. Meanwhile, in a revealing series of encounters and experiences, the two sets of parents become close, sharing their secrets and comparing their lives. Against the backdrop of two contrasting cultures—as well as two different generations within each culture—the the two families' interactions lead to unexpected discoveries about each other and about themselves.

北京故事生詞統計表

幕數	節數	生詞總數	必記的生詞	瞭解的生詞
	I	50	42	8
1		6	5	1
2		6	6	0
3		3	2	1
4		11	7	4
5		24	22	2
	II	46	36	10
6-8		0	0	0
9		24	16	8
10-11		0	0	0
12		6	6	0
13		16	14	2
	III	45	41	4
14		0	0	
15		14	12	2
16-17		0	0	0
18		1	1	0
19		22	20	2
20-21		0	0	0
22		8	8	0
	IV	50	44	6
23		14	14	0
24		12	10	2
25		11	10	1
26		0	0	0
27		13	10	3
	V	44	34	10
28		23	13	10
29		4	4	0
30		1	1	0
31		0	0	0
32		3	3	0

32		3	3	0
33		8	8	0
34		1	1	0
35		4	4	0
	VI	50	49	1
36		34	33	1
37		16	16	0
	VII	39	36	3
38		10	9	1
39		7	6	1
40		22	21	1
	VIII	40	32	8
41		8	8	0
42-43		0	0	0
44		17	16	1
45		0	0	0
46		15	8	7
	IX	33	27	6
47		31	25	6
48		0	0	0
49		0	0	0
50		2	2	0
	X	26	20	6
51		9	6	3
52		2	2	0
53		5	4	1
54		0	0	0
55		0	0	0
56		6	5	1
57		0	0	0
58		2	1	1
59		1	1	0
60		1	1	0
61		0	0	0
總計		423	361	62

電影常用語

Film Terminology

	製片	zhìpiàn	producer
	製片廠	zhìpiàn chǎng	movie studio
	編劇	biānjù	screen—writer; to write a play
	導演	dǎoyǎn	director
	人員	rényuán	personnel, staff
	攝影	shèyǐng	photography
	錄音	lùyīn	recording
	作曲	zuòqǔ	musical composition
	剪輯	jiǎnjí	(film) editing
)	照明	zhàomíng	lighting
	音響	yīnxiǎng	sound effects
;	化裝	huàzhuāng	make—up
;	服裝	fúzhuāng	costumes
⌐	道具	dàojù	props
)	佈景	bùjǐng	stage setting
;	指揮	zhǐhuī	(music) conductor
'	演奏	yǎnzòu	instrumental performance
;	演員	yǎnyuán	actor
)	男主角	nán zhǔjue	leading actor
)	女主角	nǔ zhǔjue	leading lady
⌐	對白	duìbái	dialogue

电影常用语

Film Terminology

制片	zhìpiàn	producer
制片厂	zhìpiàn chǎng	movie studio
编剧	biānjù	screen-writer; to write a play
导演	dǎoyǎn	director
人员	rényuán	personnel, staff
摄影	shèyǐng	photography
录音	lùyīn	recording
作曲	zuòqǔ	musical composition
剪辑	jiǎnjí	(film) editing
照明	zhàomíng	lighting
音响	yīnxiǎng	sound effects
化装	huàzhuāng	make-up
服装	fúzhuāng	costumes
道具	dàojù	props
布景	bùjǐng	stage setting
指挥	zhǐhuī	(music) conductor
演奏	yǎnzòu	instrumental performance
演员	yǎnyuán	actor
男主角	nán zhǔjue	leading actor
女主角	nǚ zhǔjue	leading lady
对白	duìbái	dialogue

人物表
Characters

方先生	Fāng xiānsheng	四十多歲，華僑，某電腦公司的高級職員
方太太	Fāng tàitai	四十多歲，華僑，不會説中國話
方保羅	Fāng Bǎoluó	美國高中學生
趙先生	Zhào xiānsheng	五十多歲，中國離休高幹
趙太太	Zhào tàitai	五十多歲，方先生的姐姐
趙莉莉	Zhào Lìli	中國高中三年級學生
張小娟	Zhāng Xiǎojuān	中國高中三年級學生，莉莉的好同學
劉先生	Liú xiānsheng	已經退休的英語教師
劉一達	Liú Yìdá	劉先生的兒子，待業青年
于載華	Yú Zàihuá	一達的好朋友，也是待業青年
教練	jiàoliàn	北海業餘體校的教練
老師	lǎoshī	某英語補習班的老師
Neil		某電腦公司的職員，方先生的同事
Wilson		某電腦公司的副經理，方先生的老板
Linda		美國高中學生，保羅的女朋友

人物表
Characters

方先生	Fāng xiānsheng	四十多岁，华侨，某电脑公司的高级职员
方太太	Fāng tàitai	四十多岁，华侨，不会说中国话
方保罗	Fāng Bǎoluó	美国高中学生
赵先生	Zhào xiānsheng	五十多岁，中国离休高干
赵太太	Zhào tàitai	五十多岁，方先生的姐姐
赵莉莉	Zhào Lìli	中国高中三年级学生
张小娟	Zhāng Xiǎojuān	中国高中三年级学生，莉莉的好同学
刘先生	Liú xiānsheng	已经退休的英语教师
刘一达	Liú Yìdá	刘先生的儿子，待业青年
于载华	Yú Zàihuá	一达的好朋友，也是待业青年
教练	jiàoliàn	北海业余体校的教练
老师	lǎoshī	某英语补习班的老师
Neil		某电脑公司的职员，方先生的同事
Wilson		某电脑公司的副经理，方先生的老板
Linda		美国高中学生，保罗的女朋友

對白

第一節 Section One

第一幕到第五幕 Scene 1 to Scene 5

While watching the first five scenes of the movie, keep in mind the themes introduced by environment and activity. Some things to consider are the services and employees at the bathhouse, the appeal of Coca-Cola, the significance of ping-pong and the view of Chang'an Avenue. Try to guess four potential themes of this film.

第一幕 ---去澡堂打零工

師傅： 洗澡？

一達： 不洗。

師傅： 幹甚麼？

一達： 臨時工。

師傅： 來。

師傅： 欸，給你。

一達： 欸，你歇歇。

第二幕 ---載華請一達喝可口可樂

顧客： 多少錢一瓶兒？

店員： 七毛。

顧客： 喲，太貴了。

一達： 咱們這臨時工一天才掙一塊五啊！

一達： 這是甚麼呀？

載華： 哈哈！哈哈！哈哈！

对白

第一节 Section One

第一幕到第五幕　Scene 1 to Scene 5

While watching the first five scenes of the movie, keep in mind the themes introduced by environment and activity. Some things to consider are the services and employees at the bathhouse, the appeal of Coca-Cola, the significance of ping-pong and the view of Chang'an Avenue. Try to guess four potential themes of this film.

第一幕 ---去澡堂打零工

师傅：　洗澡？

一达：　不洗。

师傅：　干甚么？

一达：　临时工。

师傅：　来。

师傅：　欸，给你。

一达：　欸，你歇歇。

第二幕 ---载华请一达喝可口可乐

顾客：　多少钱一瓶儿？

店员：　七毛。

顾客：　哟，太贵了。

一达：　咱们这临时工一天才挣一块五啊！

一达：　这是甚么呀？

载华：　哈哈！哈哈！哈哈！

1

第三幕 ---在北海業餘體校

教練：　欸，快！

第四幕 ---　小娟在街上碰見了莉莉

小娟：　莉莉，莉莉。

莉莉：　張小娟，幹嘛去啊？

小娟：　昨兒你怎麼沒去英語班上課啊？禮拜一你也沒有去？

莉莉：　我爸爸說給我找個私人教師。那補習班兒特沒勁兒。

小娟：　你下次一定得來補習班幫我對付對付。

莉莉：　究竟是哪個老想勾搭你呀？

小娟：　就是老坐在後邊兒上課盡打盹兒的。

莉莉：　上課打盹的有好幾個呢，是高的還是矮的？

小娟：　不高。

莉莉：　欸，我到家了。再見。

小娟：　再見。

第五幕 ---在趙家

趙先生：唉，新車就這麼糟蹋。莉莉，今兒你是怎麼了？啊！喔唷，唉，你看，我這個鳥兒給嚇壞了。

趙太太：瞧，莉莉這是甚麼？

莉莉：　咱們甚麼時候上青島啊？上次您說的？

趙太太：哦，讓我看看。噢，安排的是七月份。

莉莉：　剛好是高考的那個月。那我怎麼去呀？

趙太太：要想去青島，要你爸爸重新安排不就是了。欸，快瞧瞧這信，你舅舅說甚麼呀？

莉莉：　My dearest niece,...

趙太太：那是甚麼意思？

莉莉：　It has been a long time...

2

第三幕 ---在北海业余体校

教练：　　欸，快！

第四幕 ---　小娟在街上碰见了莉莉

小娟：　　莉莉，莉莉。
莉莉：　　张小娟，干嘛去啊？
小娟：　　昨儿你怎么没去英语班上课啊？礼拜一你也没有去？
莉莉：　　我爸爸说给我找个私人教师。那补习班儿特没劲儿。
小娟：　　你下次一定得来补习班帮我对付对付。
莉莉：　　究竟是哪个老想勾搭你呀？
小娟：　　就是老坐在后边儿上课尽打盹儿的。
莉莉：　　上课打盹的有好几个呢，是高的还是矮的？
小娟：　　不高。
莉莉：　　欸，我到家了。再见。
小娟：　　再见。

第五幕 ---在赵家

赵先生：唉，新车就这么糟蹋。莉莉，今儿你是怎么了？啊！喔唷，唉，你看，
　　　　我这个鸟儿给吓坏了。
赵太太：瞧，莉莉这是甚么？
莉莉：　　咱们甚么时候上青岛啊？上次您说的？
赵太太：哦，让我看看。噢，安排的是七月份。
莉莉：　　刚好是高考的那个月。那我怎么去呀？
赵太太：要想去青岛，要你爸爸重新安排不就是了。欸，快瞧瞧这信，你舅舅说
　　　　甚么呀？
莉莉：　　My dearest niece,...
赵太太：那是甚么意思？
莉莉：　　It has been a long time...

2

趙太太：欸，大概是甚麼意思？

莉莉：　你別催嘛，我這查都查不過來了呢。

趙太太：你舅舅啊，出去三十多年了，八成連中國字兒都不會寫了。出去的時候
　　　　剛十歲，光調皮不愛唸書，可是捅婁子的事兒沒對兒。

莉莉：　我琢磨出來了。舅舅他們就要來北京。

趙太太：欸，我說，弟弟又說這會兒要來了。

赵太太：欸，大概是甚么意思？

莉莉：　你别催嘛，我这查都查不过来了呢。

赵太太：你舅舅啊，出去三十多年了，八成连中国字儿都不会写了。出去的时候刚十岁，光调皮不爱念书，可是捅娄子的事儿没对儿。

莉莉：　我琢磨出来了。舅舅他们就要来北京。

赵太太：欸，我说，弟弟又说这会儿要来了。

生詞及例句

生辭

*1	澡堂	zǎotáng	(public) bath house
2	打工	dǎgōng	to do (informal speech limited to odd jobs or short term labor)
3	零工	línggōng	temporary, part time, or short term work
4	臨時工	línshí gōng	temporary worker
5	欸	ài↘	short, sharp-toned interjection at beginning of sentence, used to get someones's attention, answer or show recognition
6	歇歇	xiēxie	休息一會兒，to take a short rest or break

例句

A 在中國，從前男人常到澡堂去洗澡 xǐzǎo (to take a bath) 一方面
因爲中國從前家裏多半沒有洗澡間 xǐzǎojiān (bathroom) 一方面
因爲在澡堂裡洗澡很舒服。在那兒不但可以洗熱水澡，有人給搓澡
cuōzǎo (give sb a rubdown with a damp towel at his bath)，
修脚 xiūjiǎo (to pare toe-nails)　而且可以跟朋友談話、談買賣、

生词及例句

第一幕

生词

*1	澡堂	zǎotáng	(public) bath house
2	打工	dǎgōng	to do (informal speech limited to odd jobs or short term labor)
3	零工	línggōng	temporary, part time, or short term work
4	临时工	línshí gōng	temporary worker
5	欸	ài ↘	short, sharp-toned interjection at beginning of sentence, used to get someones's attention, answer or show recognition
6	歇歇	xiēxie	休息一会儿，to take a short rest or break

例句

A 在中国，从前男人常到澡堂去洗澡 xǐzǎo (to take a bath) 一方面
因为中国从前家裏多半没有洗澡间 xǐzǎojiān (bathroom) 一方面
因为在澡堂里洗澡很舒服。在那儿不但可以洗热水澡，有人给搓澡
cuōzǎo (give sb a rubdown with a damp towel at his bath)，
修脚 xiūjiǎo (to pare toe-nails) 而且可以跟朋友谈话、谈买卖、

喝茶甚麼的。

B　你在哪兒做事？

我在一個飯館兒打零工。

那個工作是長期的還是臨時的？

是臨時的。

甚麼人在那兒做臨時工？

多半是學生在那兒打工。

C　你太累了，歇歇吧。我來做。

欸，好。謝謝。

第二幕

生詞

1	請	qǐng	to treat someone, to invite, please
2	喲	yo↗	interjection at beginning of phrase used to show surprise
3	可口可樂	kě-kǒu-kě-lè	Coca-Cola (palatable and fun)
4	咱們	zánmen	all of us, we all (inclusive of listener)
5	掙	zhèng	to earn, to make (money)
6	哈哈！	hāhā!	(laughter)

例句：

A　咱們去看電影兒好嗎？

好啊！上次你請我，這次該我請你了。請你請莉莉一塊兒去。

哈哈！太好了。

B　可口可樂是美國的汽水，你喜歡喝嗎？

C　你打零工一個禮拜可以掙多少錢？

掙十幾塊錢。

喝茶甚么的。

B　你在哪儿做事？

我在一个饭馆儿打零工。

那个工作是长期的还是临时的？

是临时的。

甚么人在那儿做临时工？

多半是学生在那儿打工。

C　你太累了，歇歇吧。我来做。

欸，好。谢谢。

第二幕

生词

1	请	qǐng	to treat someone, to invite, please
2	哟	yo↗	interjection at beginning of phrase used to show surprise
3	可口可乐	kě-kǒu-kě-lè	Coca-Cola (palatable and fun)
4	咱们	zánmen	all of us, we all (inclusive of listener)
5	挣	zhèng	to earn, to make (money)
6	哈哈！	hāhā!	(laughter)

例句：

A　咱们去看电影儿好吗？

好啊！上次你请我，这次该我请你了。请你请莉莉一块儿去。

哈哈！太好了。

B　可口可乐是美国的汽水，你喜欢喝吗？

C　你打零工一个礼拜可以挣多少钱？

挣十几块钱。

5

哟，就掙那麼一點兒錢啊！

第三幕

生詞

1	業餘	yèyú	amateur, recreational; sparetime
*2	體校	tǐ xiào	physical education school, recreation center for youth
3	教練	jiàoliàn	coach

例句

A　教打球是你的正式工作嗎？

　　不是，我是一個業餘的教練。我業餘沒事兒的時候，就教人打球。

B　"體校"是甚麼意思？

　　"體校"是"體育學校"的簡稱 jiancheng (abbreviation)。

第四幕

1	幹嘛？	gànma ?	What are you doing? What's up? Why?
*2	私人教師	sīrén jiàoshī	private teacher, tutor
*3	補習班	bǔxí bān	a class for supplementary schooling; a school to take care of drop-outs; an extensionary school
4	特	tè	很, (short for 特別) really, particularly, extremely
*5	沒勁兒	méijìng(r)	boring (as an activity); to have little energy, lifeless
6	對付	duìfu	to handle, to deal with
7	究竟	jiūjìng	到底, after all; the very truth

哟，就挣那么一点儿钱啊！

第三幕

生词

1	业余	yèyú	amateur, recreational; sparetime
*2	体校	tǐxiào	physical education school, recreation center for youth
3	教练	jiàoliàn	coach

例句

A 教打球是你的正式工作吗？

　不是，我是一个业余的教练。我业余没事儿的时候，就教人打球。

B "体校"是甚么意思？

　"体校"是"体育学校"的简称 Jiancheng (abbreviation).

第四幕

1	干嘛？	gànma？	What are you doing? What's up? Why?
*2	私人教师	sīrén jiàoshī	private teacher, tutor
*3	补习班	bǔxí bān	a class for supplementary schooling; a school to take care of drop-outs; an extensionary school
4	特	tè	很，(short for 特别) really, particularly, extremely
*5	没劲儿	méijìn(r)	boring (as an activity); to have little energy, lifeless
6	对付	duìfu	to handle, to deal with
7	究竟	jiūjìng	到底，after all; the very truth

			(used in a question, often followed by a verb, e.g., 你究竟懂不懂？)
*8	勾搭	gōuda	to flirt with, to harrass, to lure
9	盡	jìn	always, continually
*10	打盹兒	dǎdǔn(r)	to doze off, to fall asleep or nap
11	矮	ǎi	short, not tall, petite

例句

A　老師，"幹嘛去" 這個詞兒的意思我不懂。
　　"幹嘛去" 在這兒是 "到哪兒去" 或是 "去做甚麼" 的意思。有時候
　　"幹嘛" 是 "爲甚麼" 的意思。比方：你幹嘛不説話？

B　孩子的功課不好，父母請了一個私人教師在家給孩子補習。

C　有的學生放學以後還到補習班去補習。

D　老師，請問，"特沒勁兒" 是甚麼意思。
　　這是北京方言，"特" 是 "特別，非常" 的意思，"沒勁兒" 是
　　"沒意思" 的意思"。所以 "特沒勁兒" 就是 "特別，或非常沒意思。"

E　那個男孩子想勾搭你女兒，你最好想個辦法對付他。
　　我女兒已經大了，要是她不喜歡他，她自己應該知道怎麽對付他。
　　她究竟還小，你應該告訴她。

F　我説了半天，你究竟懂不懂啊？

G　我昨天晚上沒睡覺，所以上課的時候老打盹兒。

H　那兩個人一個高一個矮。你究竟是喜歡高個兒的還是矮個兒的？
　　那還用説，當然是高個兒的。

第五幕

生詞

1	唉	àiゝ	interjection with a long-low tone expressing exasperation, disapproval, or sadness

			(used in a question, often followed by a verb, e.g., 你究竟懂不懂？)
*8	勾搭	gōuda	to flirt with, to harrass, to lure
9	尽	jìn	always, continually
*10	打盹儿	dǎdǔn(r)	to doze off, to fall asleep or nap
11	矮	ǎi	short, not tall, petite

例句

A 老师，"干嘛去"这个词儿的意思我不懂。
　"干嘛去"在这儿是"到哪儿去"或是"去做甚么"的意思。有时候
　"干嘛"是"为甚么"的意思。比方：你干嘛不说话？

B 孩子的功课不好，父母请了一个私人教师在家给孩子补习。

C 有的学生放学以后还到补习班去补习。

D 老师，请问，"特没劲儿"是甚么意思。
　这是北京方言，"特"是"特别，非常"的意思，"没劲儿"是
　"没意思"的意思"。所以"特没劲儿"就是"特别，或非常没意思。"

E 那个男孩子想勾搭你女儿，你最好想个办法对付他。
　我女儿已经大了，要是她不喜欢他，她自己应该知道怎么对付他。
　她究竟还小，你应该告诉她。

F 我说了半天，你究竟懂不懂啊？

G 我昨天晚上没睡觉，所以上课的时候老打盹儿。

H 那两个人一个高一个矮。你究竟是喜欢高个儿的还是矮个儿的？
　那还用说，当然是高个儿的。

第五幕

生词

1	唉	ài↘	interjection with a long-low tone expressing exasperation, disapproval, or sadness

7

2	糟蹋	zāota	to waste or ruin something; to rape women or treat savagely
3	嚇壞了	xià huàile	to frighten to death, to shock
4	青島	Qīngdǎo	Qingdao, a port city in Shandong
5	哦	o↗	high-rising interjection which shows sudden realization, surprise
6	讓	ràng	to let, to allow
7	噢	o↘	short-falling toned interjection showing understanding or acknowledgement
8	安排	ānpái	to plan, to schedule, to arrange
9	七月份	qí yuè fèn	during July
10	高考	gāo kǎo	annual college entrance exam (used in mainland China, called 大學入學考試 in Taiwan)
11	重新	chóngxīn	to do again, redo
12	不就是了	bújiùshìle	as simple as that,...and that's it, no problem
13	瞧	qiáo	看, look!
14	舅舅	jiùjiu	mother's brother
15	催	cuī	to urge, to rush someone to do something more quickly
16	嘛	ma	particle at end of sentence which shows assertion or affirmation
17	查	chá	to look up (in dictionary), to scan
18	八成	bā-chéng	大概, probably; 80%
*19	光	guāng	只, 就, only, just
20	調皮	tiáopí	naughty, mischievous
*21	捅婁子	tǒnglóuzi	make mischief, screw up, get into trouble
22	沒對兒	méi duì(r)	to be unmatched (in a talent)

8

2	糟蹋	zāota	to waste or ruin something; to rape women or treat savagely
3	吓坏了	xià huàile	to frighten to death, to shock
4	青岛	Qīngdǎo	Qingdao, a port city in Shandong
5	哦	o ↗	high-rising interjection which shows sudden realization, surprise
6	让	ràng	to let, to allow
7	噢	o ↘	short-falling toned interjection showing understanding or acknow-ledgement
8	安排	ānpái	to plan, to schedule, to arrange
9	七月份	qí yuè fèn	during July
10	高考	gāo kǎo	annual college entrance exam (used in mainland China, called 大学入学考试 in Taiwan)
11	重新	chóngxīn	to do again, redo
12	不就是了	bújiùshìle	as simple as that,...and that's it, no problem
13	瞧	qiáo	看, look!
14	舅舅	jiùjiu	mother's brother
15	催	cuī	to urge, to rush someone to do something more quickly
16	嘛	ma	particle at end of sentence which shows assertion or affirmation
17	查	chá	to look up (in dictionary), to scan
18	八成	bā-chéng	大概, probably; 80%
*19	光	guāng	只, 就, only, just
20	调皮	tiáopí	naughty, mischievous
*21	捅娄子	tǒnglóuzi	make mischief, screw up, get into trouble
22	没对儿	méi duì(r)	to be unmatched (in a talent)

8

| 23 | 琢磨 | zuómo | to figure out; to ponder |
| 24 | 我說 | wǒ-shuō | I say (often used before a comment or to catch someone's attention) |

例句

A　吃的東西很貴，別糟蹋。

B　在中國，高中畢業以後，要是你想上大學，就得參加高考。

C　唉！這次高考又沒考上。
　　沒關係。明年再考一次不就是了。
　　唉！又得重新預備。

D　讓她慢慢查字典，別催她！你越催她越查不到。
　　哦，好。我不催她了。

E　"八成"在這兒是"大概"的意思。

F　老師不喜歡那個學生，八成是因為他太調皮。上課的時候愛說話。

G　小孩子不能光唸書不玩兒嘛！

H　噢？他今天又捅了一個婁子，把一個酒盃打破了。

I　我琢磨半天才琢磨出來這個句子的意思。

| 23 | 琢磨 | zuómo | to figure out; to ponder |
| 24 | 我说 | wǒ-shuō | I say (often used before a comment or to catch someone's attention) |

例句

A 吃的东西很贵，别糟蹋。

B 在中国，高中毕业以后，要是你想上大学，就得参加高考。

C 唉！这次高考又没考上。

没关系。明年再考一次不就是了。

唉！又得重新预备。

D 让她慢慢查字典，别催她！你越催她越查不到。

哦，好。我不催她了。

E "八成"在这儿是"大概"的意思。

F 老师不喜欢那个学生，八成是因为他太调皮。上课的时候爱说话。

G 小孩子不能光念书不玩儿嘛！

H 噢？他今天又捅了一个娄子，把一个酒杯打破了。

I 我琢磨半天才琢磨出来这个句子的意思。

練習一

一　課堂討論

1　電影剛開始的時候，爲甚麼特別有下面的幾個鏡頭？
　（1）　公共澡堂。
　（2）　練習乒乓球。
　（3）　北京的街道。
　（4）　可口可樂。

2　電影兒裏那兩個男孩子叫甚麼名字？那兩個女孩子叫甚麼名字？

3　是那兩個男孩子家還是女孩子家有錢？你怎麼知道？

4　請你說一說中國公共澡堂裏的情形。

5　其他？

二　問答題

1　爲甚麼一達跟載華到公共澡堂去？

2　打零工一個鐘頭掙多少錢？可口可樂一瓶多少錢？

3　你想一達喜歡喝美國的可口可樂嗎？你怎麼知道？

4　小娟要莉莉幫她甚麼忙？爲甚麼？

5　莉莉爲甚麼這兩天沒到補習班去？

6　趙先生爲甚麼說莉莉糟蹋東西？

练习一

一　课堂讨论

1　电影刚开始的时候，为甚么特别有下面的几个镜头？

　　（1）　公共澡堂。

　　（2）　练习乒乓球。

　　（3）　北京的街道。

　　（4）　可口可乐。

2　电影儿裏那两个男孩子叫甚么名字？那两个女孩子叫甚么名字？

3　是那两个男孩子家还是女孩子家有钱？你怎么知道？

4　请你说一说中国公共澡堂裏的情形。

5　其他？

二　问答题

1　为甚么一达跟载华到公共澡堂去？

2　打零工一个钟头挣多少钱？可口可乐一瓶多少钱？

3　你想一达喜欢喝美国的可口可乐吗？你怎么知道？

4　小娟要莉莉帮她甚么忙？为甚么？

5　莉莉为甚么这两天没到补习班去？

6　赵先生为甚么说莉莉糟蹋东西？

10

7　趙家七月份要到哪兒去？莉莉爲甚麼説那個月不好？

8　趙家接到一封從哪兒來的信？那封信上説甚麼？

9　莉莉看得懂英文信嗎？你怎麼知道？

10　要是你看不太懂中文信，你怎麼辦？

三　造句

1　歇歇：

2　掙：

3　業餘：

4　對付：

5　究竟：

6　嚇壞了：

7　安排：

8　重新：

9　催：

10　調皮：

7　赵家七月份要到哪儿去？莉莉为甚么说那个月不好？

8　赵家接到一封从哪儿来的信？那封信上说甚么？

9　莉莉看得懂英文信吗？你怎么知道？

10　要是你看不太懂中文信，你怎么办？

三　造句

1　歇歇：

2　挣：

3　业余：

4　对付：

5　究竟：

6　吓坏了：

7　安排：

8　重新：

9　催：

10　调皮：

四　自由發揮

　　請你寫出來中國澡堂的情形：

四　自由发挥

请你写出来<u>中国</u>澡堂的情形：

對白
第二節 Section Two
第六幕到第十三幕　Scene 6 to Scene 13

In this section, consider the emphasis on contrasts. Keep in mind differences in social status, attitude, and relationships. What tensions are introduced? How does culture seem to dictate behavior in conflict resolution? In friendship?

第六幕 ---在美國加州一高級住宅區

Neil:　　Oh, that's it! Damn it. I've been trying to debug that program for the whole week. My God!

方先生：I don't know about your god, but my god should be a smart, handsome Chinese guy who is perfectly circumcised.

Neil:　　Perfectly?!

方先生：Perfectly.

第七幕 ---在方家

方先生：啊，牛肉麵。Thank you, dear.
　　　　What do you have to say about your report card, son?

保羅：　Nothing.

方太太：Professor Chuang just called. He said you only showed up for his Chinese One class once.

保羅：　I have been going to Chinese class ever since I can remember. You know what? I never got to watch Bugs Bunny.

对白

第二节 Section Two

第六幕到第十三幕　Scene 6 to Scene 13

In this section, consider the emphasis on contrasts. Keep in mind differences in social status, attitude, and relationships. What tensions are introduced? How does culture seem to dictate behavior in conflict resolution? In friendship?

第六幕 ---在美国加州一高级住宅区

Neil:　　Oh, that's it! Damn it. I've been trying to debug that program for the whole week. My God!

方先生:　I don't know about your god, but my god should be a smart, handsome Chinese guy who is perfectly circumcised.

Neil:　　Perfectly?!

方先生:　Perfectly.

第七幕 ---在方家

方先生:　啊，牛肉面。Thank you, dear.
　　　　　What do you have to say about your report card, son?

保罗:　　Nothing.

方太太:　Professor Chuang just called. He said you only showed up for his Chinese One class once.

保罗:　　I have been going to Chinese class ever since I can remember. You know what? I never got to watch Bugs Bunny.

方先生： Son, nobody should deny his own cultural background. Although we sent you to Chinese school every year, but you still don't speak Chinese!

第八幕 ---在方力群工作的電腦公司

第九幕 ---在劉家的大雜院兒

載華： 叔叔，苦瓜，您嚐嚐。

劉先生：我苦了一輩子，不吃這個。

載華： 一達歇着呢？

載華： 哥兒們，醒過來行不行？死啦？嘿，真沒氣了，這回哥兒們真沒氣了。

一達： 他媽的！手往哪兒擱過來着，他媽的一股邪味兒。

載華： 沒味兒呀，咱這手，看哥兒們這手長得多有福氣，就是想碰的都摸不上搆不着呢。欸，美國現在誰唱歌最有名呀？

一達： Luciano Pavarotti.

載華： 哦！誰呀？你説個短的行不行？是不是就是唱那個冰冷的小脚兒的那個？

一達： 冰涼的小手。

載華： 唱唱！

一達： （唱歌...）

鄰居： 別唱了！嚇得我們小三都尿炕了。

第十幕 ---在美國的一個健身房

方太太： We've been preparing for a trip to Peking for the last five years. He has a standing invitation from his sister in Peking, and the China Computer Society. I even took him seriously once and took a class in Chinese.

女同事： I thought you spoke Chinese.

方太太： Can't you tell? I'm an American!

方先生： Son, nobody should deny his own cultural background. Although we sent you to Chinese school every year, but you still don't speak Chinese!

第八幕 ---在方力群工作的电脑公司

第九幕 ---在刘家的大杂院儿

载华：　　叔叔，苦瓜，您尝尝。
刘先生：我苦了一辈子，不吃这个。
载华：　　一达歇着呢？
载华：　　哥儿们，醒过来行不行？死啦？嗨，真没气了，这回哥儿们真没气了。
一达：　　他妈的！手往哪儿搁过来着，他妈的一股邪味儿。
载华：　　没味儿呀，咱这手，看哥儿们这手长得多有福气，就是想碰的都摸不上构不着呢。欸，美国现在谁唱歌最有名呀？
一达：　　Luciano Pavarotti.
载华：　　哦！谁呀？你说个短的行不行？是不是就是唱那个冰冷的小脚儿的那个？
一达：　　冰凉的小手。
载华：　　唱唱！
一达：　　（唱歌...）
邻居：　　别唱了！吓得我们小三都尿炕了。

第十幕 ---在美国的一个健身房

方太太：We've been preparing for a trip to Peking for the last five years. He has a standing invitation from his sister in Peking, and the China Computer Society. I even took him seriously once and took a class in Chinese.
女同事：I thought you spoke Chinese.
方太太：Can't you tell? I'm an American!

第十一幕 ---在電腦公司

方先生: I don't know about our president, Wilson. He's so indecisive.

Neil: Ah, I mean it's only natural. After all, you've been in charge of that PC division for the past four years now.

方先生: I only did the technical part of the project, you have done all this administrative work. Haven't you?

Neil: Yeah, well somebody has to mop up the floors. Not that I enjoy it, I was told to do it.

方先生: Hey Jimmy! How ya' doin'?

同事: Hey Leo. Congratulations, I heard the good news about you becoming the new director of the PC division. You really deserve it.

方先生: Thank you, but it hasn't been official yet.

第十二幕 ---在某英語補習班

老師: Today we are going to have new lesson. 今天咱們要講第二十二課, "My Hometown" "我的家鄉"。我先把課文念一遍, 大家要注意聽啊, 這個, 注意聽的時候啊, 要想想中文是甚麼意思, 看能懂多少。My hometown is a beautiful place. It stands beside a wide river...

載華: 別睡覺！

一達: 不睡不成啊, 這書我已經讀過三遍了。

小娟: 你看, 他睡着了。

莉莉: （笑）。

載華: 回頭下課咱們一定得找那倆説話去。

一達: 説甚麼呀？

載華: 説借筆記本啊。

老師: 懂不懂啊？

第十一幕 ---在电脑公司

方先生： I don't know about our president, Wilson. He's so indecisive.

Neil： Ah, I mean it's only natural. After all, you've been in charge of that PC division for the past four years now.

方先生： I only did the technical part of the project, you have done all this administrative work. Haven't you?

Neil： Yeah, well somebody has to mop up the floors. Not that I enjoy it, I was told to do it.

方先生： Hey Jimmy! How ya' doin'?

同事： Hey Leo. Congratulations, I heard the good news about you becoming the new director of the PC division. You really deserve it.

方先生： Thank you, but it hasn't been official yet.

第十二幕 ---在某英语补习班

老师： Today we are going to have new lesson. 今天咱们要讲第二十二课，"My Hometown" "我的家乡"。我先把课文念一遍，大家要注意听啊，这个，注意听的时候啊，要想想中文是甚么意思，看能懂多少。My hometown is a beautiful place. It stands beside a wide river...

载华： 别睡觉！

一达： 不睡不成啊，这书我已经读过三遍了。

小娟： 你看，他睡着了。

莉莉： （笑）。

载华： 回头下课咱们一定得找那俩说话去。

一达： 说甚么呀？

载华： 说借笔记本啊。

老师： 懂不懂啊？

小娟：　　就是後邊兒那倆。

莉莉：　　不怕他們。

老師：　　你們懂不懂呀？"river" 甚麼意思？"river".

第十三幕 ---在教室外邊兒

載華：　　你好！

莉莉：　　你好個甚麼呀？又不是美國人，見了生人還得你好你好的。

載華：　　"五講四美"，講禮貌啊！

莉莉：　　欵，是不是你？

載華：　　不，不是我。

莉莉：　　不是你，哼，就是你。

一達：　　我，... 沒有啊！

莉莉：　　反正你們倆，幹嘛老是想勾搭張小娟？討厭。

載華：　　看您說的，都是同班同學還有不說話的？

莉莉：　　誰跟你們同學？胡同兒裏的。

載華：　　胡同兒裏的怎麼了？您不也（是住在）胡同兒裏的嗎？

莉莉：　　你想怎麼樣？

載華：　　交個朋友。瞧，這哥兒們多帥，英文說得溜着呢，正經的，還會唱歌劇。哥兒們，露一手，那叫甚麼來着？"爬坡兒露底"？

一達：　　不，Pavarotti.

16

小娟： 就是后边儿那俩。

莉莉： 不怕他们。

老师： 你们懂不懂呀？"river"甚么意思？"river".

第十三幕 ---在教室外边儿

载华： 你好！

莉莉： 你好个甚么呀？又不是<u>美国</u>人，见了生人还得你好你好的。

载华： "五讲四美"，讲礼貌啊！

莉莉： 欸，是不是你？

载华： 不，不是我。

莉莉： 不是你，哼，就是你。

一达： 我，... 没有啊！

莉莉： 反正你们俩，干嘛老是想勾搭<u>张小娟</u>？讨厌。

载华： 看您说的，都是同班同学还有不说话的？

莉莉： 谁跟你们同学？胡同儿裏的。

载华： 胡同儿裏的怎么了？您不也（是住在）胡同儿裏的吗？

莉莉： 你想怎么样？

载华： 交个朋友。瞧，这哥儿们多帅，英文说得溜着呢，正经的，还会唱歌剧。哥儿们，露一手，那叫甚么来着？"爬坡儿露底"？

一达： 不，Pavarotti.

生詞及例句

第九幕

1	叔叔	shūshu	father's younger brother, a male friend of one's parents
*2	苦瓜	kǔ guā	bitter melon, a kind of cucumber
3	嚐嚐	chángchang	to try a little (for taste or smell); taste it
*4	歇着	xiēzhe	to be resting, taking a nap
5	苦	kǔ	bitter
6	一輩子	yí beìzi	for (my) whole life, a lifetime of
*7	哥兒們	gērmen	pal or pals, buddy
8	醒過來	xǐng guólai	to wake up, recover from hangover
9	嘿	hei ↗	less polite interjection used to get someone's attention
*10	沒氣兒	méi qì(r)	not breathing
*11	他媽的！	tā-māde!	his mother! (a curse used casually in disgust)
12	擱	gē	放, to put, to place
13	一股	yì gǔ	a whiff (measure word for smell)
*14	邪味兒	xiéwèi(r)	nasty odor
15	多	duó	how, quite (how wonderful!); many
16	福氣	fúqi	to have a rich life in the sense of having many children, enough money, and a long life
17	摸	mō	to touch, to feel (with hand)

17

生词及例句

第九幕

1	叔叔	shūshu	father's younger brother, a male friend of one's parents
*2	苦瓜	kǔ guā	bitter melon, a kind of cucumber
3	尝尝	chángchang	to try a little (for taste or smell); taste it
*4	歇着	xiēzhe	to be resting, taking a nap
5	苦	kǔ	bitter
6	一辈子	yí bèizi	for (my) whole life, a lifetime of
*7	哥儿们	gērmen	pal or pals, buddy
8	醒过来	xǐng guòlai	to wake up, recover from hangover
9	嘿	hei↗	less polite interjection used to get someone's attention
*10	没气儿	méi qì(r)	not breathing
*11	他妈的！	tā-māde!	his mother! (a curse used casually in disgust)
12	搁	gē	放, to put, to place
13	一股	yì gǔ	a whiff (measure word for smell)
*14	邪味儿	xiéwèi(r)	nasty odor
15	多	duó	how, quite (how wonderful!); many
16	福气	fúqi	to have a rich life in the sense of having many children, enough money, and a long life
17	摸	mō	to touch, to feel (with hand)

18	摳	gōu	to reach out with hand
19	來着	láizhe	huh? what did you say? (a particle indicating need to be reminded of something)
20	冰冷	bīnglěng	frozen, freezing (to feel very cold)
21	冰涼	bīngliáng	ice cold
22	嚇	xià	scare, frighten
*23	尿	niào	to urinate; urine
*24	炕	kàng	a brick platform bed that can be heated from beneath (usually found in North China)

例句

A 爸爸的弟弟是你的親叔叔。有時候朋友的爸爸或是爸爸的朋友也叫叔叔。

B 請嚐嚐這個瓜甜不甜？
　嘿，你真會開玩笑，這是苦瓜，當然是苦的，怎麼能甜呢？

C 他的生活真苦，一輩子都沒有錢，吃了不少苦。

D 我叫了他半天才把他叫醒過來。

E 他死了。你看，他沒氣兒了。

F 你把我的書擱在哪兒了？
　擱在桌子上了。

G 你剛才說甚麼來着？我沒聽見。請再說一次。

H 誰抽煙了？一股煙味兒？

I "邪味兒"是不好聞的味兒。比方說：他很久沒洗澡，所以身上有一股邪味兒。

J 你看，那個小姐長得怎麼樣？
　她的眼睛長得很好看，可是鼻子長得不好看。

K 您真有福氣，那麼大年紀了，身體這麼健康，又有錢，又有那麼好的孩子。

L 那個東西你放得太高了，我摳不着。

18

18	构	gòu	to reach out with hand
19	来着	láizhe	huh? what did you say ? (a particle indicating need to be reminded of something)
20	冰冷	bīnglěng	frozen, freezing (to feel very cold)
21	冰凉	bīngliáng	ice cold
22	吓	xià	scare, frighten
*23	尿	niào	to urinate; urine
*24	炕	kàng	a brick platform bed that can be heated from beneath (usually found in North China)

例句

A 爸爸的弟弟是你的亲叔叔。有时候朋友的爸爸或是爸爸的朋友也叫叔叔。

B 请尝尝这个瓜甜不甜？

嘿，你真会开玩笑，这是苦瓜，当然是苦的，怎么能甜呢？

C 他的生活真苦，一辈子都没有钱，吃了不少苦。

D 我叫了他半天才把他叫醒过来。

E 他死了。你看，他没气儿了。

F 你把我的书搁在哪儿了？

搁在桌子上了。

G 你刚才说甚么来着？我没听见。请再说一次。

H 谁抽烟了？一股烟味儿？

I "邪味儿"是不好闻的味儿。比方说：他很久没洗澡，所以身上有一股邪味儿。

J 你看，那个小姐长得怎么样？

她的眼睛长得很好看，可是鼻子长得不好看。

K 您真有福气，那么大年纪了，身体这么健康，又有钱，又有那么好的孩子。

L 那个东西你放得太高了，我构不着。

站在椅子上不就搆得着了嗎？

M 我八成病了。你摸摸我的手冰冷/ 冰涼。

N 老虎來了，把那個孩子嚇哭了。

O 要是自己不知道，夜裡小便在牀上叫尿炕或是尿床。

第十二幕

生詞

1	家鄉	jiāxiāng	hometown
2	課文	kèwén	text of a lesson
3	睡覺	shuìjiào	to sleep, to go to bed (for various activities)
4	回頭	huítóu	一會兒, in a second, in a flash; to turn one's head
5	倆	liǎ	two people (must be used after 我們，你們，她們，他們，這 or 那)
6	筆記本	bǐjìběn	notebook

例句

A "家鄉"是一個人出生的地方，也可以說"故鄉"或是"老家"。

B 你們先預備生詞跟課文，回頭我來問你們問題。

C 上課的時候你應該注意聽老師講話，不應該回頭看後面。

D "倆"有兩個的意思：一個是"兩個的意思。"比方說：他們倆是好朋友。
一個是"很少的意思。"比方說：就這倆錢怎麼够？

E 下課的時候，有的學生在筆記本上寫筆記，有的在書上畫畫兒，有的在
睡覺。

站在椅子上不就构得着了吗？

M 我八成病了。你摸摸我的手冰冷／冰凉。

N 老虎来了，把那个孩子吓哭了。

O 要是自己不知道，夜里小便在床上叫尿炕或是尿床。

第十二幕

生词

1	家乡	jiāxiāng	hometown
2	课文	kèwén	text of a lesson
3	睡觉	shuìjiào	to sleep, to go to bed (for various activities)
4	回头	huítóu	一会儿, in a second, in a flash; to turn one's head
5	俩	liǎ	two people (must be used after 我们, 你们, 她们, 他们, 这 or 那)
6	笔记本	bǐjì běn	notebook

例句

A "家乡"是一个人出生的地方，也可以说"故乡"或是"老家"。

B 你们先预备生词跟课文，回头我来问你们问题。

C 上课的时候你应该注意听老师讲话，不应该回头看后面。

D "俩"有两个的意思：一个是"两个的意思。"比方说：他们俩是好朋友。
一个是"很少的意思。"比方说：就这俩钱怎么够？

E 下课的时候，有的学生在笔记本上写笔记，有的在书上画画儿，有的在
睡觉。

19

第十三幕

生詞

1	生人	shēng rén	不認識的人，someone you don't really know, stranger
*2	五講四美	wǔ-jiǎng-sì-měi	"Five Stresses and Four Points of Beauty" --a national political campaign starting February 8, 1981, emphasizing decorum, manners, hygiene, discipline and morals; beautification of mind, language, behavior, and the environment.
3	講	jiǎng	to pay attention to, stress (especially for etiquette); to speak or give a speech
4	禮貌	lǐmào	etiquette, manners, courtesy
5	不是...就是	bùshi...jiùshi	if it's not...then it is
6	哼	heng↘	heavy nasal interjection showing disgust
7	反正	fǎnzhèng	in any case, no matter what
8	討厭	tǎoyàn	disgusting, dislike, yuk (usage and strength defined by context and intonation)
9	同班	tóng bān	classmate
10	胡同兒	hútòng(r)	alley (usually refers to a poor neighborhood)
11	交	jiāo	to make (friends); to hand in
12	帥	shuài	handsome (used only for males)
*13	溜着呢！	liūzhene!	fluent, flowing (compliment on

第十三幕

生词

1	生人	shēng rén	不认识的人，someone you don't really know, stranger
*2	五讲四美	wǔ-jiǎng-sì-měi	"Five Stresses and Four Points of Beauty" --a national political campaign starting February 8, 1981, emphasizing decorum, manners, hygiene, discipline and morals; beautification of mind, language, behavior, and the environment.
3	讲	jiǎng	to pay attention to, stress (especially for etiquette); to speak or give a speech
4	礼貌	lǐmào	etiquette, manners, courtesy
5	不是...就是	búshi...jiùshi	if it's not...then it is
6	哼	heng ˅	heavy nasal interjection showing disgust
7	反正	fǎnzhèng	in any case, no matter what
8	讨厌	tǎoyàn	disgusting, dislike, yuk (usage and strength defined by context and intonation)
9	同班	tóng bān	classmate
10	胡同儿	hútòng(r)	alley (usually refers to a poor neighborhood)
11	交	jiāo	to make (friends); to hand in
12	帅	shuài	handsome (used only for males)
*13	溜着呢！	liùzhene!	fluent, flowing (compliment on

20

			one's foreign language skill)
14	正經	zhèngjing	seriously; serious; very proper or respectable
15	歌劇	gējù	opera
16	露一手兒	lòuyishǒu(r)	show us, show off a little

例句

A 中國人平常只跟熟人打招呼，不跟生人打招呼。

B 因爲有很多人不講禮貌，所以政府提倡"五講四美。"

C 他每天不是唸書就是寫報告，真用功。

D 不管你去不去，反正我要去。

E "討厭"是不喜歡的意思。比方説：學生都討厭考試。

F 我們是同班的同學，你怎麼説話那麼沒有禮貌？
　哼，誰説同學就得客氣啊？

G 我們住在同一個胡同兒，你怎麼能不認識我呢？
　哼，討厭，誰認識你？

H 她最近交了一個男朋友，長得很帥。

I 他的中國話説得溜着呢，跟中國人一樣。

J 你別開玩笑，説正經的，你究竟會不會唱歌劇？

K 他是一個正經人，不會做勾搭別人太太那種不正經的事。

L 你明天露一手，把你的拿手好菜做給我們嚐嚐。

			one's foreign language skill)
14	正经	zhèngjing	seriously; serious; very proper or respectable
15	歌剧	gējù	opera
16	露一手儿	lòuyishǒu(r)	show us, show off a little

例句

A 中国人平常只跟熟人打招呼，不跟生人打招呼。

B 因为有很多人不讲礼貌，所以政府提倡"五讲四美。"

C 他每天不是念书就是写报告，真用功。

D 不管你去不去，反正我要去。

E "讨厌"是不喜欢的意思。比方说：学生都讨厌考试。

F 我们是同班的同学，你怎么说话那么没有礼貌？

　哼，谁说同学就得客气啊？

G 我们住在同一个胡同儿，你怎么能不认识我呢？

　哼，讨厌，谁认识你？

H 她最近交了一个男朋友，长得很帅。

I 他的中国话说得溜着呢，跟中国人一样。

J 你别开玩笑，说正经的，你究竟会不会唱歌剧？

K 他是一个正经人，不会做勾搭别人太太那种不正经的事。

L 你明天露一手，把你的拿手好菜做给我们尝尝。

練習二

一　課堂討論

1　第六幕開始的時候是在甚麼地方？

2　中國的街上跟美國有甚麼大的不同？

3　方先生跟 Neil 一邊兒慢跑一邊兒談甚麼？

4　方家有幾口人？趙家呢？兩家父母對孩子的看法有甚麼相同的地方，有甚麼不相同的地方？

5　劉家住的地方跟趙家住的地方有甚麼不一樣？

6　方太太跟她的朋友在健身房談甚麼事？為甚麼她的朋友想她會說中國話？

7　其他？

二　問答題

1　保羅喜歡學中文嗎？他學了多久中文了？

2　方先生說為甚麼保羅得學中文。

3　為甚麼劉先生不要吃苦瓜？

4　你想一達跟載華高興嗎？為甚麼？

5　方太太為甚麼要學中文？

6　方先生在哪兒做事？他的同事想他應該不應該做主任？

练习二

一　课堂讨论

1　第六幕开始的时候是在甚么地方？

2　中国的街上跟美国有甚么大的不同？

3　方先生跟 Neil 一边儿慢跑一边儿谈甚么？

4　方家有几口人？赵家呢？两家父母对孩子的看法有甚么相同的地方，
　　有甚么不相同的地方？

5　刘家住的地方跟赵家住的地方有甚么不一样？

6　方太太跟她的朋友在健身房谈甚么事？为甚么她的朋友想她会说
　　中国话？

7　其他？

二　问答题

1　保罗喜欢学中文吗？他学了多久中文了？

2　方先生说为甚么保罗得学中文。

3　为甚么刘先生不要吃苦瓜？

4　你想一达跟载华高兴吗？为甚么？

5　方太太为甚么要学中文？

6　方先生在哪儿做事？他的同事想他应该不应该做主任？

7　在英文補習班上課的時候莉莉，小娟，一達，跟載華在做甚麼？

8　爲甚麼載華對莉莉跟小娟很有禮貌？

9　你想莉莉是真的很討厭那兩個男孩子嗎？

10　載華說一達是甚麼樣的人？

三　造句

1　嚐嚐：

2　摸：

3　搆

4　課文

5　睡覺

6　禮貌：

7　不是...就是：

8　不管...反正：

9　討厭：

10　交：

7　在英文补习班上课的时候莉莉，小娟，一达，跟载华在做甚么？

8　为甚么载华对莉莉跟小娟很有礼貌？

9　你想莉莉是真的很讨厌那两个男孩子吗？

10　载华说一达是甚么样的人？

三　造句

1　尝尝：

2　摸：

3　构

4　课文

5　睡觉

6　礼貌：

7　不是...就是：

8　不管...反正：

9　讨厌：

10　交：

23

四 翻譯

1 Your professor just called, he said you only showed up for his Chinese class once.

2 We sent you to Chinese school every year, but you still don't speak Chinese!

3 We've been preparing for a trip to Peking for the last five years.

4 I thought you spoke Chinese.
Can't you tell? I'm an American!

5 My hometown is a beautful place. It stands beside a wide river.

五 自由發揮

從第六幕到第十三幕，你有甚麼不懂的地方嗎？請你寫出幾個問題來。

四 翻译

1 Your professor just called, he said you only showed up for his Chinese class once.

2 We sent you to Chinese school every year, but you still don't speak Chinese!

3 We've been preparing for a trip to Peking for the last five years.

4 I thought you spoke Chinese.
   Can't you tell? I'm an American!

5 My hometown is a beautful place. It stands beside a wide river.

五 自由发挥

从第六幕到第十三幕，你有甚么不懂的地方吗？请你写出几个问题来。

對白

第三節 Section Three

第十四幕到第二十二幕 Scene 14 to Scene 22

At least four themes are developed in this third section; what are they? As you watch these scenes, think about why those themes were chosen. How are the families in San Francisco and Beijing different?

第十四幕 ---在電腦公司

Wilson: Well, Jim has already discussed our income for the year. Keep it up gentlemen, and Francis. Uh, our PC computer, Compricot, has been very competitive thanks to Leo, Neil, and their fellow workers. It therefore should come as no surprise that we've decided to establish a new PC division. The new director of this PC division is... Mr. Neil Mahoney. Compricot's inventor, Mr. Leo Fang, has been promoted to headquarters as senior member of our technical staff to our senior vice-president.

方先生: Five years ago you told me I didn't have enough experience to be director. Now, Neil Mahoney has less experience than I had five years ago.

Wilson: There were other considerations.

方先生: Like what?

Wilson: Well, such as youth. I mean Neil's younger than you.

方先生: Oh, so you're telling me I'm too old for this job.

Wilson: No, I don't mean that at all. Now look, Neil has lots of good qualities. Now listen to me Leo!

方先生: Neil, Neil doesn't know the system well.

25

对白
第三节 Section Three

第十四幕到第二十二幕 Scene 14 to Scene 22

At least four themes are developed in this third section; what are they? As you watch these scenes, think about why those themes were chosen. How are the families in San Francisco and Beijing different?

第十四幕 ---在电脑公司

Wilson: Well, Jim has already discussed our income for the year. Keep it up gentlemen, and Francis. Uh, our PC computer, Compricot, has been very competitive thanks to Leo, Neil, and their fellow workers. It therefore should come as no surprise that we've decided to establish a new PC division. The new director of this PC division is... Mr. Neil Mahoney. Compricot's inventor, Mr. Leo Fang, has been promoted to headquarters as senior member of our technical staff to our senior vice-president.

方先生: Five years ago you told me I didn't have enough experience to be director. Now, Neil Mahoney has less experience than I had five years ago.

Wilson: There were other considerations.

方先生: Like what?

Wilson: Well, such as youth. I mean Neil's younger than you.

方先生: Oh, so you're telling me I'm too old for this job.

Wilson: No, I don't mean that at all. Now look, Neil has lots of good qualities. Now listen to me Leo!

方先生: Neil, Neil doesn't know the system well.

25

Wilson: He'll learn. He'll learn. Look, you have a real good job, very high up in the company, hardly any hassle.

方先生: Let me tell you what I think you're thinking. You don't believe the Chinaman is good enough to be the director. That's what you're thinking.

第十五幕 ---在劉家大雜院

婦女： 小三兒，回來，刷了碗再去看電視！

小三兒： 欵，就來。

趙先生： 沒錯兒，就是這兒。劉先生啊，老劉先生啊！

劉先生： 喲！老趙，你怎麼來了？也不言語一聲，你看，這是多少年啦！

趙先生： 我這來求您幫忙來了。這是我閨女。

劉先生： 都成大人啦！你瞧。屋裏坐，屋裏坐。我這兒除了髒亂，就是擠了。

趙先生： 是啊，我這閨女，別的功課都還可以，就是英語差點兒。應付高考還有點兒難。求您來教教。

劉先生： 我這英語啊，也是老式英語啦，再說水平也有限。

趙先生： 哪兒啊，全北京誰不知道除了許國璋就數您劉老先生了。

第十六幕 ---在劉家上課

劉先生： 這是甚麼時態？If you want to study English well, you must study hard. That means memorizing the dictionary. When I was young, I used to memorize fifty words a day. 在我年輕的時候，我一天背五十個生字。But some person doesn't want to do this. I don't know why. Okay, excuse me.

第十七幕 ---在方家客廳

保羅： Let's get married. Now.

Linda: Your father might come home early.

Wilson: He'll learn. He'll learn. Look, you have a real good job, very high up in the company, hardly any hassle.

方先生: Let me tell you what I think you're thinking. You don't believe the Chinaman is good enough to be the director. That's what you're thinking.

第十五幕 ---在刘家大杂院

妇女： 小三儿，回来，刷了碗再去看电视！

小三儿：欸，就来。

赵先生：没错儿，就是这儿。刘先生啊，老刘先生啊！

刘先生：哟！老赵，你怎么来了？也不言语一声，你看，这是多少年啦！

赵先生：我这来求您帮忙来了。这是我闺女。

刘先生：都成大人啦！你瞧。屋裏坐，屋裏坐。我这儿除了脏乱，就是挤了。

赵先生：是啊，我这闺女，别的功课都还可以，就是英语差点儿。应付高考还有点儿难。求您来教教。

刘先生：我这英语啊，也是老式英语啦，再说水平也有限。

赵先生：哪儿啊，全北京谁不知道除了许国璋就数您刘老先生了。

第十六幕 ---在刘家上课

刘先生：这是甚么时态？If you want to study English well, you must study hard. That means memorizing the dictionary. When I was young, I used to memorize fifty words a day. 在我年轻的时候，我一天背五十个生字。But some person doesn't want to do this. I don't know why. Okay, excuse me.

第十七幕 ---在方家客厅

保罗： Let's get married. Now.

Linda： Your father might come home early.

保羅：　Pretend he's in China now.

Linda: Paul, are you really going to China this summer?

保羅：　Actually, I don't think we're ever really going to get there. Know what?

Linda: What?

保羅：　I don't think he really wants to go.

Linda: Why not?

保羅：　Because reality often produces disappointments.　Funny old man.

方先生：Hey, everybody, I have an announcement to make!　We are going to have a vacation! One month or even longer. How's that?

保羅：　Pop, for real?

方先生：You bet. We're all going. You deserve it, I deserve it. We finally deserve it.

保羅：　You mean like... all four of us? Oh.

第十八幕 ---在北海業餘體校

莉莉：　可以嘛，你現在球打得不錯嘛！

一達：　哪兒啊！我這還退步好多了呢。

第十九幕 ---在圓明園廢墟

莉莉：　Bay, B-A-Y.

一達：　島嶼。

莉莉：　Yees land.

一達：　甚麼？

莉莉：　I-S-LAND, iceland.

一達：　No, 念 island.

莉莉：　誰說的？

一達：　我爸爸。他還能錯？

莉莉：　真丟人，念大白字兒。哼，哼。我看你爸爸暗地裏還頂疼你的。

保罗：　Pretend he's in China now.

Linda：　Paul, are you really going to China this summer?

保罗：　Actually, I don't think we're ever really going to get there. Know what?

Linda：　What?

保罗：　I don't think he really wants to go.

Linda：　Why not?

保罗：　Because reality often produces disappointments. Funny old man.

方先生：Hey, everybody, I have an announcement to make! We are going to have a vacation! One month or even longer. How's that?

保罗：　Pop, for real?

方先生：You bet. We're all going. You deserve it, I deserve it. We finally deserve it.

保罗：　You mean like... all four of us? Oh.

第十八幕 ---在北海业余体校

莉莉：　可以嘛，你现在球打得不错嘛！

一达：　哪儿啊！我这还退步好多了呢。

第十九幕 ---在圆明园废墟

莉莉：　Bay, B-A-Y.

一达：　岛屿。

莉莉：　Yees land.

一达：　甚么？

莉莉：　I-S-LAND, iceland.

一达：　No，念 island.

莉莉：　谁说的？

一达：　我爸爸。他还能错？

莉莉：　真丢人，念大白字儿。哼，哼。我看你爸爸暗地裏还顶疼你的。

一達： 可他老覺得我沒考上大學，沒出息。就算我考取了大學，我的本事和他一樣大，又怎麼樣呢？還不是一樣住大雜院？欸，聽我的。

"Four score and seven years ago, our fathers brought forth on this continent a new nation, a new nation considered in levity and dedicated to the proposition that all men are created equal. We here highly resort that this nation under God shall have not new spurts of freedom and that government of the people, by the people, for the people should not perish from the eeearth."

莉莉： 哈，哈，哈。

一達： 我剛才念的獨白怎麼樣？

莉莉： 挺好。

一達： 有沒有總統的感覺？

莉莉： 作記者當然好啊，可以派到世界各地去逛，逛完了再寫幾篇感想。人家還給登出來。

一達： 想得挺美，人家憑甚麼專送你去世界各地呀？

莉莉： 不送我送誰？

一達： 你說的對。

莉莉： 你想幹甚麼？

一達： 幹甚麼都可以，只要能上個大學，將來有個好單位，分上一個單元就可以了。

莉莉： 嗯。

第二十幕 ---在方家客廳

Linda: Um, I'm leaving. Hi, Mr. Fang, have a pleasant trip.

方先生：Bye, Linda. ... What's wrong, Romeo?

保羅： Father, give me a break. Who's playing?

方先生：Forty-niners and the Broncos. Hey, I thought you'd stop seeing Linda.

保羅： I will... when I'm in China.

一达：　可他老觉得我没考上大学，没出息。就算我考取了大学，我的本事和他一样大，又怎么样呢？还不是一样住大杂院？欸，听我的。

"Four score and seven years ago, our fathers brought forth on this continent a new nation, a new nation considered in levity and dedicated to the proposition that all men are created equal. We here highly resort that this nation under God shall have not new spurts of freedom and that government of the people, by the people, for the people should not perish from the eeearth."

莉莉：　哈，哈，哈。

一达：　我刚才念的独白怎么样？

莉莉：　挺好。

一达：　有没有总统的感觉？

莉莉：　作记者当然好啊，可以派到世界各地去逛，逛完了再写几篇感想。人家还给登出来。

一达：　想得挺美，人家凭甚么专送你去世界各地呀？

莉莉：　不送我送谁？

一达：　你说的对。

莉莉：　你想干甚么？

一达：　干甚么都可以，只要能上个大学，将来有个好单位，分上一个单元就可以了。

莉莉：　嗯。

第二十幕 ---在方家客厅

Linda:　Um, I'm leaving. Hi, Mr. Fang, have a pleasant trip.

方先生：Bye, Linda. ... What's wrong, Romeo?

保罗：　Father, give me a break. Who's playing?

方先生：Forty-niners and the Broncos. Hey, I thought you'd stop seeing Linda.

保罗：　I will... when I'm in China.

方先生： What ever happened to that nice Chinese girl, Margaret Wei?

保羅： She's going out with some white guy. Why don't you like Linda as my friend? You know the only reason you don't like her is 'cause she's not Chinese.

方先生： C'mon, I never suggested anything like that.

保羅： It's true. All Chinese parents are racist.

方先生： What are you talking about? Hey!

保羅： You use the tradition and the culture to cover up the racism. Really. Why do we have to do everything the Chinese way anyway? It gets you nowhere. This is America, you know? You've lived here for so long, and you still talk with an accent.

方先生： What's wrong with my accent? I think it's rather cute!

方太太： What's the weight limit on each suitcase again?

方先生： Forty-four pounds. ... Yes, yes! Sack him!

第二十一幕 ---在方家臥房

方太太： Here's an interesting paragraph about the city of Peking. Listen, "Peking is a city..."

方先生： Peking is a city surrounded by walls, big thick walls.

方太太： What? Why?

方先生： To keep the invaders out or to confine the natives in. It is just as hard to leave the city as it is to go back.

方太太： What does your sister say in the letter?

方先生： Oh, they still didn't do anything about father's grave.

方太太： Oh no.

第二十二幕 ---在北京城裏

方先生： Where's the wall?

方太太： "The Great Wall is located sixty miles northwest of the city...

方先生： What ever happened to that nice Chinese girl, Margaret Wei?

保罗： She's going out with some white guy. Why don't you like Linda as my friend? You know the only reason you don't like her is 'cause she's not Chinese.

方先生： C'mon, I never suggested anything like that.

保罗： It's true. All Chinese parents are racist.

方先生： What are you talking about? Hey!

保罗： You use the tradition and the culture to cover up the racism. Really. Why do we have to do everything the Chinese way anyway? It gets you nowhere. This is America, you know? You've lived here for so long, and you still talk with an accent.

方先生： What's wrong with my accent? I think it's rather cute!

方太太： What's the weight limit on each suitcase again?

方先生： Forty-four pounds. ... Yes, yes! Sack him!

第二十一幕 ---在方家卧房

方太太： Here's an interesting paragraph about the city of Peking. Listen, "Peking is a city..."

方先生： Peking is a city surrounded by walls, big thick walls.

方太太： What? Why?

方先生： To keep the invaders out or to confine the natives in. It is just as hard to leave the city as it is to go back.

方太太： What does your sister say in the letter?

方先生： Oh, they still didn't do anything about father's grave.

方太太： Oh no.

第二十二幕 ---在北京城裏

方先生： Where's the wall?

方太太： "The Great Wall is located sixty miles northwest of the city...

方先生： I don't mean that wall. 同志，北京的城牆哪兒去了？

司機： 哦，北京的城牆啊，建國初期爲了要擴建首都北京，國務院下令拆除了。

方太太： "The wall of Peking city was torn down right after liberation for the purpose of expanding the nation's capital."

方先生： Geez, what do you know? China expert, eh?

方太太： The guidebook doesn't lie all the time.

方先生： Those damn highrises.

方先生： I don't mean that wall. 同志，<u>北京</u>的城墙哪儿去了？

司机： 哦，<u>北京</u>的城墙啊，建国初期为了要扩建首都<u>北京</u>，国务院下令拆除了。

方太太： "The wall of Peking city was torn down right after liberation for the purpose of expanding the nation's capital."

方先生： Geez, what do you know? China expert, eh?

方太太： The guidebook doesn't lie all the time.

方先生： Those damn highrises.

生詞及例句

第十五幕

生詞

1	刷碗	shuā wǎn	洗碗，to wash dishes
*2	言語	yányuan	say something; tell
*3	閨女	guīnü	女兒，daughter
4	髒亂	zāngluàn	dirty and messy
5	擠	jǐ	crowded
6	差點兒	chà diǎn(r)	not very good at; almost, nearly
7	應付	yìngfu	to handle, to deal with, to cope with
8	求	qiú	to beg, to ask for a favor
9	老式	lǎo shì	old-fashioned
10	水平	shuǐpíng	level of ability
11	有限	yǒu xiàn	to be limited, to have limits
12	全	quán	whole; entirely
13	除了... 就是	chúle...jiùshi	not only...also..., apart from ... just...
14	數	shǔ	considered, counted as

例句

A 要是每天吃了飯不必刷碗就好了。

B "不言語"是北京話，有兩個意思：一個是"不説話"的意思。比方説：
你爲甚麼坐在那兒一聲也不言語？
一個是"不告訴"的意思。比方説：

31

生词及例句

生词

1	刷碗	shuā wǎn	洗碗, to wash dishes
*2	言语	yányuan	say something; tell
*3	闺女	guīnü	女儿, daughter
4	脏乱	zāngluàn	dirty and messy
5	挤	jǐ	crowded
6	差点儿	chà diǎn(r)	not very good at; almost, nearly
7	应付	yìngfu	to handle, to deal with, to cope with
8	求	qiú	to beg, to ask for a favor
9	老式	lǎo shì	old-fashioned
10	水平	shuǐpíng	level of ability
11	有限	yǒu xiàn	to be limited, to have limits
12	全	quán	whole; entirely
13	除了...就是	chúle...Jiùshi	not only...also..., apart from ... just...
14	数	shǔ	considered, counted as

例句

A 要是每天吃了饭不必刷碗就好了。

B "不言语"是北京话，有两个意思：一个是"不说话"的意思。比方说：

你为甚么坐在那儿一声也不言语？

一个是"不告诉"的意思。比方说：

你不舒服了，怎麼不早言語一聲？

我帶你去看大夫。

C　"閨女"是"女兒"的意思。比方説：我有兩個閨女，一個兒子。

D　他每天除了吃飯就是睡覺，一點兒正經事都不做。

E　紐約的中國城又擠又髒亂。

F　"差點兒"有兩個意思。一個是"差不多"的意思。比方説：我今天
　　　差點兒遲到了（可是沒遲到。）
　　　一個是"不太好"的意思。比方説：我的中
　　　文不錯，可是英文差點兒。

G　我的中文水平不好，怕應付不了這次的考試．求你給我補習補習好嗎？

H　我們的錢有限，買不起彩電 cǎi diàn (color TV)，只好買一個黑白的。

I　在我們全校的同學裏數你的英語最好了。

哪兒啊，比我好的人多着呢，那能數得到我！

第十八幕

生詞

1　退步　　　　　　tuì bù　　　　　to regress, fall back in skill

例句

A　我的中國話不但沒進步，而且退步了不少。

不會吧！

第十九幕

生詞

1　丟人　　　　　diūrén　　　　lose face, to be embarrassed

你不舒服了，怎么不早言语一声？

我带你去看大夫。

C　"闺女"是"女儿"的意思。比方说：我有两个闺女，一个儿子。

D　他每天除了吃饭就是睡觉，一点儿正经事都不做。

E　纽约的中国城又挤又脏乱。

F　"差点儿"有两个意思。一个是"差不多"的意思。比方说：我今天
　　差点儿迟到了（可是没迟到。）
　　一个是"不太好"的意思。比方说：我的中
　　文不错，可是英文差点儿。

G　我的中文水平不好，怕应付不了这次的考试．求你给我补习补习好吗？

H　我们的钱有限，买不起彩电 cǎi diàn (color TV)，只好买一个黑白的。

I　在我们全校的同学里数你的英语最好了。

哪儿啊，比我好的人多着呢，那能数得到我！

第十八幕

生词

1　退步　　　　　　tuì bù　　　　　to regress, fall back in skill

例句

A　我的中国话不但没进步，而且退步了不少。

不会吧！

第十九幕

生词

1　丢人　　　　　　diūrén　　　　　lose face, to be embarrassed

32

2	念白字	niàn báizì	to mispronounce or mispell
3	暗地	àndì	secretly
4	頂	dǐng	很，very; top, peak
5	疼	téng	to love (usually parental love); to be in pain
6	沒出息	méi chūxi	to lack promise, have no future
*7	大雜院兒	dà záyuàn(r)	shack; many small families' homes connected by one courtyard, often created from one big house and in poor condition
*8	獨白	dúbái	monologue; speech
9	總統	zǒngtǒng	president
10	感覺	gǎnjué	to feel, feeling
11	記者	jìzhě	journalist, reporter
12	派	pài	to send (people), to delegate
13	世界	shìjiè	the world
14	逛	guàng	travel, browse, window-shop
15	感想	gǎnxiǎng	thoughts
16	登	dēng	to publish an article in a newspaper or magazine; to climb
17	挺	tǐng	very, quite
18	憑	píng	based on, according to
19	專	zhuān	especially
20	單位	dānwèi	work unit
21	單元	dānyuán	unit (here refers to an apartment)
22	嗯	n/ng ˇ	yes (interjection at beginning of sentence showing agreement)

例句

A "丢人"是"丢臉，沒面子，不好意思"的意思。

2	念白字	niàn báizì	to mispronounce or mispell
3	暗地	àndì	secretly
4	顶	dǐng	很, very; top, peak
5	疼	téng	to love (usually parental love); to be in pain
6	没出息	méi chūxi	to lack promise, have no future
*7	大杂院儿	dà záyuàn(r)	shack; many small families' homes connected by one courtyard, often created from one big house and in poor condition
*8	独白	dúbái	monologue; speech
9	总统	zǒngtǒng	president
10	感觉	gǎnjué	to feel, feeling
11	记者	jìzhě	journalist, reporter
12	派	pài	to send (people), to delegate
13	世界	shìjiè	the world
14	逛	guàng	travel, browse, window-shop
15	感想	gǎnxiǎng	thoughts
16	登	dēng	to publish an article in a newspaper or magazine; to climb
17	挺	tǐng	very, quite
18	凭	píng	based on, according to
19	专	zhuān	especially
20	单位	dānwèi	work unit
21	单元	dānyuán	unit (here refers to an apartment)
22	嗯	n/ng ⌄	yes (interjection at beginning of sentence showing agreement)

例句

A "丢人"是"丢脸，没面子，不好意思"的意思。

B 把"字念錯了"就是念"白字"，比方説你把"還錢"的
"還（huán）"字念成"還（hái）"字了。

C 一達暗地裏喜歡莉莉，不敢告訴她。

D 我很喜歡登山。你呢？
我也頂喜歡登山。因爲在山頂上可以看見不同的世界。

E 天下沒有不疼孩子的父母。要是孩子不好，他們就很頭疼。

F 他考不上大學不一定沒出息。他還可以做別的事。

G 這件衣服那麽難看，就算你送我我也不要。

H 就算你天天打他，又有甚麽用呢？他還是不喜歡念書。

I 莉莉覺得一達念的獨白不錯。

J 美國前任總統是雷根，現任總統是布希。

K 別人打你，罵你的時候你有甚麽感覺？
打我的時候我感覺疼，罵我的時候我感覺非常生氣。

L 要是我有錢我就到世界各地去逛逛。你呢？
我去逛街，買東西，吃館子。

M 這本書看完了以後，我打算把我的感想寫出來，寄給紐約時報
"New York Times"希望能給我登出來。

N 你的單位有那麽多人要房子住，憑甚麽專分給你一個單元？
因爲我家有十口人。
嗯，説的也有道理。

第二十二幕

生詞

1	城牆	chéng qiáng	city wall
2	建國	jiàn guó	establish a nation (here referring to the P.R.C. in 1949)
3	初期	chū qī	early stage, beginning of
4	擴建	kuò jiàn	to expand, to develop

34

B 把"字念错了"就是念"白字"，比方说你把"还钱"的
  "还（huán）"字念成"还（hái）"字了。

C 一达暗地裏喜欢莉莉，不敢告诉她。

D 我很喜欢登山。你呢？
  我也顶喜欢登山。因为在山顶上可以看见不同的世界。

E 天下没有不疼孩子的父母。要是孩子不好，他们就很头疼。

F 他考不上大学不一定没出息。他还可以做别的事。

G 这件衣服那么难看，就算你送我我也不要。

H 就算你天天打他，又有甚么用呢？他还是不喜欢念书。

I 莉莉觉得一达念的独白不错。

J 美国前任总统是雷根，现任总统是布希。

K 别人打你，骂你的时候你有甚么感觉？
  打我的时候我感觉疼，骂我的时候我感觉非常生气。

L 要是我有钱我就到世界各地去逛逛。你呢？
  我去逛街，买东西，吃馆子。

M 这本书看完了以后，我打算把我的感想写出来，寄给纽约时报
  "New York Times"希望能给我登出来。

N 你的单位有那么多人要房子住，凭甚么专分给你一个单元？
  因为我家有十口人。
  嗯，说的也有道理。

第二十二幕

生词

1	城墙	chéng qiáng	city wall
2	建国	jiàn guó	establish a nation (here referring to the P.R.C. in 1949)
3	初期	chū qī	early stage, beginning of
4	扩建	kuò jiàn	to expand, to develop

34

5	首都	shǒudū	capital of a nation
6	國務院	guówù yuàn	the state council
7	下令	xià lìng	to give a formal order
8	拆除	chāichú	to destroy, to tear down

例句

A 從前在北京有很高很大的城牆，1949年共產黨建立中華人民共和國以後，爲了把北京城擴建得大一點兒就把城牆給拆除了。
是誰下令拆除的？
國務院。

B 從前中國國務院的總理是周恩來，現在呢？

35

5	首都	shǒudū	capital of a nation
6	国务院	guówù yuàn	the state council
7	下令	xià lìng	to give a formal order
8	拆除	chāichú	to destroy, to tear down

例句

A 从前在北京有很高很大的城墙，1949年共产党建立中华人民共和国
以后，为了把北京城扩建得大一点儿就把城墙给拆除了。
是谁下令拆除的？
国务院。

B 从前中国国务院的总理是周恩来，现在呢？

練習三

一 課堂討論

1 方先生想他沒能做主任的原因是甚麼？這一幕是想要說明在美國種族歧視 zhǒngzú qíshì (racism) 的問題嗎？你想美國有種族歧視的問題嗎？

2 那麼多人在大雜院做甚麼？這一幕的目的是甚麼？

3 在美國男孩子跟女孩子交朋友的情形跟中國有甚麼不同？有甚麼相同？

4 在美國的中國的父母對孩子交異性 yìxìng (opposite sex)朋友有甚麼看法？

5 現在的中國跟方先生離開的時候有甚麼不同？

6 其他？

二 問答題

1 方先生為甚麼很生氣？ Mr. Wilson 說為甚麼 Neil 應該做主任？方先生想是為甚麼？

2 院子裏那些人在看甚麼？你想他們真的懂歌劇嗎？

3 趙先生為甚麼要去找劉先生？

4 方先生為甚麼決定要到中國去了？誰邀請 yāoqǐng (invite) 他們去？

5 一達最大的希望是甚麼？為甚麼考上大學那麼要緊？

练习三

一　课堂讨论

1　方先生想他没能做主任的原因是甚么？这一幕是想要说明在美国种族歧视 zhǒngzú qíshì (racism) 的问题吗？你想美国有种族歧视的问题吗？

2　那么多人在大杂院做甚么？这一幕的目的是甚么？

3　在美国男孩子跟女孩子交朋友的情形跟中国有甚么不同？有甚么相同？

4　在美国的中国的父母对孩子交异性 yìxìng (opposite sex)朋友有甚么看法？

5　现在的中国跟方先生离开的时候有甚么不同？

6　其他？

二　问答题

1　方先生为甚么很生气？ Mr. Wilson 说为甚么 Neil 应该做主任？方先生想是为甚么？

2　院子里那些人在看甚么？你想他们真的懂歌剧吗？

3　赵先生为甚么要去找刘先生？

4　方先生为甚么决定要到中国去了？谁邀请 yāoqǐng (invite) 他们去？

5　一达最大的希望是甚么？为甚么考上大学那么要紧？

6　莉莉想做甚麼事？爲甚麼？

7　方先生希望保羅交甚麼樣的女朋友？保羅想他爸爸不喜歡 Linda 的原因是甚麼？你父母對你交異性朋友有甚麼意見嗎？

8　到外國去旅行，坐飛機可以帶多少磅行李？

9　方太太到中國去過嗎？你怎麼知道？

10　爲甚麼現在北京沒城牆了？

三　造句

1　髒亂：

2　差點兒：

3　應付：

4　水平：

5　有限：

6　除了...就是：

7　退步：

8　丟人：

9　感想：

6　莉莉想做甚么事？为甚么？

7　方先生希望保罗交甚么样的女朋友？保罗想他爸爸不喜欢 Linda
　　的原因是甚么？你父母对你交异性朋友有甚么意见吗？

8　到外国去旅行，坐飞机可以带多少磅行李？

9　方太太到中国去过吗？你怎么知道？

10　为甚么现在北京没城墙了？

三　造句

1　脏乱：

2　差点儿：

3　应付：

4　水平：

5　有限：

6　除了...就是：

7　退步：

8　丢人：

9　感想：

10 初期：

四 翻譯

1 Ten years ago you told me I didn't have enough experience to
   be director (主任). Now, Neil has less experience than I had
   five years ago.

2 Well, I mean Neil's younger than you.
   Oh, so you're telling me I'm too old for this job.

3 If you want to study Chinese well, you must study hard
   (用功). When I was young, I used to memorize (背 bèi)
   fifty words a day.

4 Paul, are you really going to China this summer?
   I don't think my father really wants to go.

5 Why don't you like Linda as my friend? You know the only
   reason you don't like her is because she's not Chinese.

五 自由發揮

1 請你說一說莉莉跟一達認識的經過。

2 你畢業以後打算作甚麼？爲甚麼？

10 初期:

四 翻译

1 Ten years ago you told me I didn't have enough experience to be director (主任). Now, Neil has less experience than I had five years ago.

2 Well, I mean Neil's younger than you.
Oh, so you're telling me I'm too old for this job.

3 If you want to study Chinese well, you must study hard (用功). When I was young, I used to memorize (背 bèi) fifty words a day.

4 Paul, are you really going to China this summer?
I don't think my father really wants to go.

5 Why don't you like Linda as my friend? You know the only reason you don't like her is because she's not Chinese.

五 自由发挥

1 请你说一说莉莉跟一达认识的经过。

2 你毕业以后打算作甚么？为甚么？

對白
第四節 Section Four
第二十三幕到第二十七幕　Scene 23 to Scene 27

As the two families come together in this section, watch how each individual reacts (including the neighbors). What presuppositions do they have about the visit? Try to explain why did the Fangs stayed at a hotel, why Mr. Zhao criticizes his wife's cooking, and What Lili means when she says she doesn't play. How do language limitations affect perception?

第二十三幕 ---在趙家大門口兒

莉莉：　媽，爸爸，來了！快點兒！

方先生：姐！

趙太太：是立群吧！欵，欵，欵，哦！這就是你姐夫。

方先生：姐夫。

趙先生：昨天去飛機場接了你們一天，怎麼今天才到呀？

方先生：飛機誤點，沒辦法。

趙太太：你好，你好，歡迎你。辛苦了吧？

方太太：Leo has told me all about you.

趙太太：莉莉，快喊舅舅！

莉莉：　舅舅。

方先生：莉莉，欵，這個兒！

趙太太：歡迎你。你好。這是你姑父。

趙先生：歡迎。

鄰居甲：這幫人哪兒的？是小日本吧？

鄰居乙：不像。像菲律賓人吧？

鄰居甲：也不像。

对白

第四节 Section Four

第二十三幕到第二十七幕　Scene 23 to Scene 27

As the two families come together in this section, watch how each individual reacts (including the neighbors). What presuppositions do they have about the visit? Try to explain why did the Fangs stayed at a hotel, why Mr. Zhao criticizes his wife's cooking, and What Lili means when she says she doesn't play. How do language limitations affect perception?

第二十三幕 ---在赵家大门口儿

莉莉：　妈，爸爸，来了！快点儿！

方先生：姐！

赵太太：是立群吧！欸，欸，欸，哦！这就是你姐夫。

方先生：姐夫。

赵先生：昨天去飞机场接了你们一天，怎么今天才到呀？

方先生：飞机误点，没办法。

赵太太：你好，你好，欢迎你。辛苦了吧？

方太太：Leo has told me all about you.

赵太太：莉莉，快喊舅舅！

莉莉：　舅舅。

方先生：莉莉，欸，这个儿！

赵太太：欢迎你。你好。这是你姑父。

赵先生：欢迎。

邻居甲：这帮人哪儿的？是小日本吧？

邻居乙：不像。像菲律宾人吧？

邻居甲：也不像。

39

鄰居甲：這家哪兒來這麼多海外關係？

鄰居乙：人家是離休高幹，甚麼沒有。

方先生：這院子跟咱們老家一樣嗎？

趙太太：完全不一樣。

第二十四幕 ---在趙家飯廳吃飯

趙太太：來來來，嚐嚐我的四喜丸子。

方先生：姐，你的手藝快趕上媽的了。

趙太太：家常飯，家常飯。嚐嚐。

趙先生：你這丸子火候差點兒。

趙太太：是嗎？莉莉，去把那個葡萄酒拿來！

莉莉：　欸。

趙太太：我不能喝白的。

趙先生：弟妹的手藝不錯吧？

方先生：He's asking about your cooking.

方太太：Oh, I only know how to cook beef noodles. 牛肉麵。

趙先生：牛肉麵做好了，可不容易啊！北京啊，可真沒有家好牛肉麵館子呢。

趙太太：欸，喝，喝，快喝！

保羅：　What do you do for fun? For fun.

莉莉：　舅舅，我怎麼學了好幾年英語還是聽不懂啊？

方先生：你們在學校玩甚麼？

莉莉：　玩兒？我們不玩兒，我們有時間還來不及學習呢。

保羅：　Do you play sports?

莉莉：　Sports? Oh，運動，哦，我喜歡打乒乓球。I play ping-pong.

保羅：　No kidding! That used to be my sport.

趙太太：還有一條魚，一鍋湯。

方先生：吃不了，別上了。

方太太：小弟，到了北京來就別住旅館了，夠貴的，打今兒起就給我搬到家裏來住。

趙先生：就是嘛！都準備好了，準備好了。

方先生：Do you wanna move in? It's all prepared.

邻居甲：这家哪儿来这么多海外关系？

邻居乙：人家是离休高干，甚么没有。

方先生：这院子跟咱们老家一样吗？

赵太太：完全不一样。

第二十四幕 ---在赵家饭厅吃饭

赵太太：来来来，尝尝我的四喜丸子。

方先生：姐，你的手艺快赶上妈的了。

赵太太：家常饭，家常饭。尝尝。

赵先生：你这丸子火候差点儿。

赵太太：是吗？莉莉，去把那个葡萄酒拿来！

莉莉：　欸。

赵太太：我不能喝白的。

赵先生：弟妹的手艺不错吧？

方先生：He's asking about your cooking.

方太太：Oh, I only know how to cook beef noodles. 牛肉面。

赵先生：牛肉面做好了，可不容易啊！北京啊，可真没有家好牛肉面馆子呢。

赵太太：欸，喝，喝，快喝！

保罗：　What do you do for fun? For fun.

莉莉：　舅舅，我怎么学了好几年英语还是听不懂啊？

方先生：你们在学校玩甚么？

莉莉：　玩儿？我们不玩儿，我们有时间还来不及学习呢。

保罗：　Do you play sports?

莉莉：　Sports? Oh, 运动，哦，我喜欢打乒乓球。I play ping-pong.

保罗：　No kidding! That used to be my sport.

赵太太：还有一条鱼，一锅汤。

方先生：吃不了，别上了。

方太太：小弟，到了北京来就别住旅馆了，都贵的，打今儿起就给我搬到家裏来住。

赵先生：就是嘛！都准备好了，准备好了。

方先生：Do you wanna move in? It's all prepared.

40

第二十五幕 ---趙先生趙太太在臥房

趙先生：你弟弟一家三口，兩口兒不會說中國話，可都會使筷子。

趙太太：你還不會使刀叉呢。

趙先生：欸，你這鼓搗甚麼呢？

趙太太：弟弟送給咱們的電毯。

趙先生：電毯，來，你躺下，我給插上電門你試試。

趙太太：我才不試呢。

趙先生：你不試，我試。

第二十六幕 ---方家在臥房裏

方太太：Leo, do you think they like me?

方先生：Sure, they're crazy about you. Believe me.

方太太：I feel like I've known them for a long time.

方先生：Of course. You all belonged to the same herd of cattle in
　　　　　your previous life.

保羅：　Dad? They don't have a shower bath here.

方先生：Too bad.

方太太：Are you warm enough Paul?

保羅：　Are you kidding? I'm hot. They have squat toilets. I don't
　　　　　think I've quite developed the leg muscles for it.

方先生：You need practice. Oh, shut up. Go to sleep will ya'?

第二十七幕 ---趙太太，趙先生在臥房

趙先生：這，<u>美國</u>人就這麼睡覺啊？電在身上呼嚕，呼嚕<u>直轉</u>，並不怎麼熱和嘛，
　　　　啊呵，熱和勁兒上來了，嘿！嗯？這是甚麼味兒啊？

趙太太：你這是胡鬧甚麼呀？

趙先生：這<u>美國</u>貨也不結實啊！欸，準是你弟弟搞錯了。他們那兒電壓和咱們

第二十五幕 ---赵先生赵太太在卧房

赵先生：你弟弟一家三口，两口儿不会说中国话，可都会使筷子。

赵太太：你还不会使刀叉呢。

赵先生：欸，你这鼓捣甚么呢？

赵太太：弟弟送给咱们的电毯。

赵先生：电毯，来，你躺下，我给插上电门你试试。

赵太太：我才不试呢。

赵先生：你不试，我试。

第二十六幕 ---方家在卧房裏

方太太：Leo, do you think they like me?

方先生：Sure, they're crazy about you. Believe me.

方太太：I feel like I've known them for a long time.

方先生：Of course. You all belonged to the same herd of cattle in
         your previous life.

保罗：　Dad? They don't have a shower bath here.

方先生：Too bad.

方太太：Are you warm enough Paul?

保罗：　Are you kidding? I'm hot. They have squat toilets. I don't
        think I've quite developed the leg muscles for it.

方先生：You need practice. Oh, shut up. Go to sleep will ya'?

第二十七幕 ---赵太太，赵先生在卧房

赵先生：这，美国人就这么睡觉啊？电在身上呼噜，呼噜直转，并不怎么热和嘛，
        啊呵，热和劲儿上来了，嘿！嗯？这是甚么味儿啊？

赵太太：你这是胡闹甚么呀？

赵先生：这美国货也不结实啊！欸，准是你弟弟搞错了。他们那儿电压和咱们

41

這兒不一樣。

趙太太：人家是電腦專家，還不懂這個。

这儿不一样。

赵太太：人家是电脑专家，还不懂这个。

生詞及例句

第二十三幕

生詞

1	姐夫	jiěfu	brother-in-law (older sister's husband)
2	接	jiē	to meet at, to pick up; to receive
3	誤點	wùdiǎn	off schedule, late (train, bus, etc.)
4	歡迎	huānyíng	to welcome
5	辛苦	xīnkǔ	to feel tired (often used in greeting a traveler because of the difficult transportation conditions); toilsome
6	喊	hǎn	to call, to greet by name (showing respect to elders); to yell, shout
7	這個兒	zhèige(r)	這個個子! look at how tall he/she is
8	姑父	gūfu	uncle (father's sister's husband)
9	幫	bāng	a gang, a group of people (informal word for group)
10	菲律賓	Fēilùbīn	Phillipines
11	海外關係	hǎiwài guānxi	foreign connections
12	離休	líxiū	retirement from civil service for CCP members who joined before 1949, no longer working, but salary and benefits are maintained
13	高幹	gāogàn	高級幹部, official, high cadre
14	老家	lǎojiā	hometown, place of birth or family origin

生词及例句

第二十三幕

生词

1	姐夫	jiěfu	brother-in-law (older sister's husband)
2	接	jiē	to meet at, to pick up; to receive
3	误点	wù diǎn	off schedule, late (train, bus, etc.)
4	欢迎	huānyíng	to welcome
5	辛苦	xīnkǔ	to feel tired (often used in greeting a traveler because of the difficult transportation conditions); toilsome
6	喊	hǎn	to call, to greet by name (showing respect to elders); to yell, shout
7	这个儿	zhèige(r)	这个个子! look at how tall he/she is!
8	姑父	gūfu	uncle (father's sister's husband)
9	帮	bāng	a gang, a group of people (informal word for group)
10	菲律宾	Fēilùbīn	Phillipines
11	海外关系	hǎiwài guānxi	foreign connections
12	离休	líxiū	retirement from civil service for CCP members who joined before 1949, no longer working, but salary and benefits are maintained
13	高干	gāo gàn	高级干部, official, high cadre
14	老家	lǎojiā	hometown, place of birth or family origin

43

例句

A 姐姐的丈夫是姐夫，那麼妹妹的丈夫呢？
　當然是妹夫了。笨蛋！ bèndàn (idiot)!

B 天氣不好，不但飛機誤點了，火車也來晚了。

C 今天有很多人到飛機場去歡迎美國總統布希。

D 為甚麼中國人常跟剛旅行回來的人説"辛苦了？"
　這也許是因為在中國從前旅行真的是很"辛苦"的關係吧！

E "舅舅"跟"姑父"有甚麼不同？
　"舅舅"是媽媽的哥哥或弟弟，"姑父"是爸爸的妹妹或姐姐的丈夫。

F 這幫人是誰啊？
　這幫人你都不認識呀！他們是"四人幫"啊！你看，那個女的就是江青。

G 他的海外關係很多，一個姐夫在美國，一個舅舅在日本，還有一個姑
　姑，姑父在菲律賓。
　為甚麼現在喜歡有海外關係？文化大革命 (Cultural Revolution)
　的時候，大家不是都怕有海外關係嗎？
　時代不同了，當然需要也不同了。這個你都不懂！

H 方先生的姐夫是離休高幹，現在雖然不做事了，可是生活還過得很好。

I 方先生的老家是北京，他離開很久了，所以回來看看。

第二十四幕

生詞

1	四喜丸子	sìxǐ wánzi	"four happiness meatballs" a dish usually of four big meatballs
2	手藝	shǒuyì	skill, talent with hands
3	趕上	gǎnshang	to catch up with, become as good as
4	家常飯	jiācháng fàn	便飯, home-cooked food, a simple mea

例句

A 姐姐的丈夫是姐夫，那么妹妹的丈夫呢？

当然是妹夫了。笨蛋！bèndàn (idiot)！

B 天气不好，不但飞机误点了，火车也来晚了。

C 今天有很多人到飞机场去欢迎美国总统布希。

D 为甚么中国人常跟刚旅行回来的人说"辛苦了？"

这也许是因为在中国从前旅行真的是很"辛苦"的关系吧！

E "舅舅"跟"姑父"有甚么不同？

"舅舅"是妈妈的哥哥或弟弟，"姑父"是爸爸的妹妹或姐姐的丈夫。

F 这帮人是谁啊？

这帮人你都不认识呀！他们是"四人帮"啊！你看，那个女的就是江青。

G 他的海外关系很多，一个姐夫在美国，一个舅舅在日本，还有一个姑

姑，姑父在菲律宾。

为甚么现在喜欢有海外关系？文化大革命 (Cultural Revolution)

的时候，大家不是都怕有海外关系吗？

时代不同了，当然需要也不同了。这个你都不懂！

H 方先生的姐夫是离休高干，现在虽然不做事了，可是生活还过得很好。

I 方先生的老家是北京，他离开很久了，所以回来看看。

第二十四幕

生词

1	四喜丸子	sìxǐ wánzi	"four happiness meatballs" a dish usually of four big meatballs
2	手艺	shǒuyì	skill, talent with hands
3	赶上	gǎnshang	to catch up with, become as good as
4	家常饭	jiācháng fàn	便饭, home-cooked food, a simple meal

*5	火候	huǒhòu	cooking time, maturity
6	葡萄酒	pútao jiǔ	wine made from grapes
7	來不及	lái-bu-jí	too late to do something
8	鍋	guō	pot for cooking, wok; a pot of
9	吃不了	chī-bu-liǎo	吃不完, to be unable to finish eating
10	上	shàng	to serve, to put on the table
*11	齁	hōu	awfully (colloquial form of 很 and 太 with very limited usage)
12	打今兒起	dǎ-jīn(r)qǐ	從今天起, from today, starting today

例句

A 趙太太的四喜丸子做得相當好，可是還趕不上她母親做的。。

B 請隨便吃，家常飯，沒甚麼好菜。

別客氣了，你做的菜比飯館兒的菜好吃多了。

C 你有沒有吃過那個飯館兒的"家常豆腐"？這個菜很不錯。

D "火候差點兒"的意思是說"不夠好或是不夠熟"的意思。

E 你喜歡喝紅葡萄酒還是米酒 (rice wine)？

都不喜歡。我喜歡喝威士忌 wèishìjì (whiskey)。

F 菜上得太快了，來不及吃了。魚等會兒再上吧！

G 你做了這麼一大鍋牛肉湯怎麼吃得了啊？

這麼多人一定吃得了。

H "齁"是"太"的意思，是北京俗話。比方說：這個湯"齁"鹹，就是這個湯"太"鹹的意思。

I "打今兒起"也是北京話，"打"是"從"，"今兒"是"今天"所以"打今兒起"是"從今天開始"的意思。

第二十五幕

生詞

*5	火候	huǒhòu	cooking time, maturity
6	葡萄酒	pútao jiǔ	wine made from grapes
7	来不及	lái-bu-jí	too late to do something
8	锅	guō	pot for cooking, wok; a pot of
9	吃不了	chī-bu-liǎo	吃不完, to be unable to finish eating
10	上	shàng	to serve, to put on the table
*11	齁	hōu	awfully (colloquial form of 很 and 太 with very limited usage)
12	打今儿起	dǎ-jīn(r)qǐ	从今天起, from today, starting today

例句

A 赵太太的四喜丸子做得相当好，可是还赶不上她母亲做的。。

B 请随便吃，家常饭，没甚么好菜。
别客气了，你做的菜比饭馆儿的菜好吃多了。

C 你有没有吃过那个饭馆儿的"家常豆腐"？这个菜很不错。

D "火候差点儿"的意思是说"不够好或是不够熟"的意思。

E 你喜欢喝红葡萄酒还是米酒 (rice wine)？
都不喜欢。我喜欢喝威士忌 wēishìjì (whiskey)。

F 菜上得太快了，来不及吃了。鱼等会儿再上吧！

G 你做了这么一大锅牛肉汤怎么吃得了啊？
这么多人一定吃得了。

H "齁"是"太"的意思，是北京俗话。比方说：这个汤"齁"咸，就是
这个汤"太"咸的意思。

I "打今儿起"也是北京话，"打"是"从"，"今儿"是"今天"所以
"打今儿起"是"从今天开始"的意思。

第二十五幕

生词

1	兩口兒	liǎng kǒu(r)	兩個人，two people
2	使	shǐ	用，to use
3	還...呢	hái...ne	not yet
4	刀叉	dāo chā	fork and knife
*5	鼓搗	gǔdao	to fiddle with, to mess with
6	電毯	diàn tǎn	electric blanket
7	躺下	tǎng xia	to lie down
8	試試	shìshi	to try, to try out or on
9	插	chā	to stick in (to plug in, to arrange flowers, to transplant rice seedlings)
10	電門	diànmén	electrical outlet
11	才...不呢	cái...bù ne	certainly does not... (emphasizes negative response opposite to expectation)

例句

A "兩口兒"就是"兩個人"的意思。比方說：我們家就有兩口人？

B "使"是"用"的意思。比方說：我還不會使毛筆寫字呢？

C "鼓搗"是北京俗話，是"弄"的意思。

D 趙太太在鼓搗她弟弟送給她的電毯。

E 你太累了，躺下來歇歇吧！

誰說我累？我才不累呢。你才累呢。

F 這間屋子的電門在哪兒？把這個電燈插上。

G 他把花兒插在哪兒了？

插在花瓶裏了。

1	两口儿	liǎng kǒu(r)	两个人，two people
2	使	shǐ	用，to use
3	还...呢	hái...ne	not yet
4	刀叉	dāo chā	fork and knife
*5	鼓捣	gǔdao	to fiddle with, to mess with
6	电毯	diàn tǎn	electric blanket
7	躺下	tǎng xia	to lie down
8	试试	shìshi	to try, to try out or on
9	插	chā	to stick in (to plug in, to arrange flowers, to transplant rice seedlings)
10	电门	diànmén	electrical outlet
11	才...不呢	cái...bù ne	certainly does not... (emphasizes negative response opposite to expectation)

例句

A "两口儿"就是"两个人"的意思。比方说：我们家就有两口人？

B "使"是"用"的意思。比方说：我还不会使毛笔写字呢？

C "鼓捣"是北京俗话，是"弄"的意思。

D 赵太太在鼓捣她弟弟送给她的电毯。

E 你太累了，躺下来歇歇吧！
谁说我累？我才不累呢。你才累呢。

F 这间屋子的电门在哪儿？把这个电灯插上。

G 他把花儿插在哪儿了？
插在花瓶裏了。

第二十七幕

生詞

*1	呼嚕	hūlu	(onomatopoeia) to move in circles
*2	直轉	zhí zhuàn	to churn around
3	並不怎麼	bìngbu zěnme	no good, not so good indeed
*4	熱和勁兒	rèhe jìn(r)	a warm and tingling feeling
5	啊哈	āhā	now I know, interjection expressing sudden realization
6	嗯?	n/ng? ↗	huh? interjection with the rising tone of a question
7	胡鬧	húnào	to fool around
8	貨	huò	東西, goods
9	結實	jiēshi	durable (goods), strong (body)
10	準是	zhǔnshì	一定是, definitely
11	搞錯了	gǎo cuòle	弄錯了, to make a mistake
12	電壓	diàn yā	voltage
13	專家	zhuānjiā	expert, specialist

例句

A 電毯插上電以後，一會兒熱和勁兒就上來了。

B 嗯？這架飛機爲甚麼在天上一直轉？

C 中國人並不一定都喜歡吃中國飯。

D 嘿！這是甚麼電影兒？一點兒意思都沒有，簡直是胡鬧嘛！

E 我們應該買本國貨，不應該買外國貨。

F 是美國貨結實還是日本貨結實？

G "準是"是"一定是"的意思。他對你那麼好，準是是一個好丈夫。

H "搞錯"是"弄錯"的意思。啊呵，你又把這件事搞錯了。

I 美國的電壓跟中國一樣嗎？

　　不一樣。美國是110，中國是220。

J 他對語言學 (linguistics) 很有研究，他是一個語言學專家。你呢？

第二十七幕

生词

*1	呼噜	hūlu	(onomatopoeia) to move in circles
*2	直转	zhí zhuàn	to churn around
3	并不怎么	bìngbu zěnme	no good, not so good indeed
*4	热和劲儿	rèhe jìn(r)	a warm and tingling feeling
5	啊哈	āhā	now I know, interjection expressing sudden realization
6	嗯？	n/ng?↗	huh? interjection with the rising tone of a question
7	胡闹	húnào	to fool around
8	货	huò	东西，goods
9	结实	jiēshi	durable (goods), strong (body)
10	准是	zhǔnshì	一定是，definitely
11	搞错了	gǎo cuòle	弄错了，to make a mistake
12	电压	diàn yā	voltage
13	专家	zhuānjiā	expert, specialist

例句

A 电毯插上电以后，一会儿热和劲儿就上来了。

B 嗯？这架飞机为甚么在天上一直转？

C 中国人并不一定都喜欢吃中国饭。

D 嘿！这是甚么电影儿？一点儿意思都没有，简直是胡闹嘛！

E 我们应该买本国货，不应该买外国货。

F 是美国货结实还是日本货结实？

G "准是"是"一定是"的意思。他对你那么好，准是是一个好丈夫。

H "搞错"是"弄错"的意思。啊呵，你又把这件事搞错了。

I 美国的电压跟中国一样吗？

不一样。美国是110，中国是220。

J 他对语言学（linguistics）很有研究，他是一个语言学专家。你呢？

47

我甚麼都不會，就會吃飯，所以我是吃飯專家。

K　　要是人的頭腦有電腦那麼快就好了。

我甚么都不会，就会吃饭，所以我是吃饭专家。

K 要是人的头脑有电脑那么快就好了。

練習四

一　課堂討論

1　方家到趙家門口的時候，爲甚麼很多人站在那兒看他們？

2　爲甚麼那些人不知道方家是哪兒的人？

3　你想趙家的鄰居喜歡趙家嗎？爲甚麼？

4　吃飯的時候趙先生説他太太的菜做的不好，你想是真的還是客氣話？
在美國先生敢在客人面前説太太的菜做的不好嗎？

5　方家在臥房的對話是要説明甚麼？

6　趙先生跟趙太太在臥房裏發生了甚麼事？

二　問答題

1　方先生是莉莉的甚麼？

2　保羅叫趙先生甚麼？

3　趙太太叫莉莉去那甚麼？趙太太説她不能喝白的是甚麼意思？

4　爲甚麼莉莉在學校不玩？

5　方家送給趙家甚麼禮物？

6　方家剛下飛機的時候住在哪兒？你怎麼知道？

7　那個電毯爲甚麼壞了？

练习四

一 课堂讨论

1 方家到赵家门口的时候，为甚么很多人站在那儿看他们？

2 为甚么那些人不知道方家是哪儿的人？

3 你想赵家的邻居喜欢赵家吗？为甚么？

4 吃饭的时候赵先生说他太太的菜做的不好，你想是真的还是客气话？
   在美国先生敢在客人面前说太太的菜做的不好吗？

5 方家在卧房的对话是要说明甚么？

6 赵先生跟赵太太在卧房里发生了甚么事？

二 问答题

1 方先生是莉莉的甚么？

2 保罗叫赵先生甚么？

3 赵太太叫莉莉去那甚么？赵太太说她不能喝白的是甚么意思？

4 为甚么莉莉在学校不玩？

5 方家送给赵家甚么礼物？

6 方家刚下飞机的时候住在哪儿？你怎么知道？

7 那个电毯为甚么坏了？

8   你想<u>趙</u>先生喜歡<u>方</u>先生嗎？你怎麼知道？

三　造句

1   怎麼...才：

2   辛苦：

3   哪兒來：

4   手藝：

5   怎麼...還是：

6   來不及：

7   打今兒起：

8   不會使（用）：

9   才不...呢：

10   並不怎麼：

四　翻譯

1   Oh, I only know how to cook beef and noodles.

2   Leo, do you think they like me?

8   你想<u>赵</u>先生喜欢<u>方</u>先生吗？你怎么知道？

三   造句

1   怎么．．．才：

2   辛苦：

3   哪儿来：

4   手艺：

5   怎么．．．还是：

6   来不及：

7   打今儿起：

8   不会使（用）：

9   才不．．．呢：

10   并不怎么：

四   翻译

1   Oh, I only know how to cook beef and noodles.

2   Leo, do you think they like me?

50

Sure, they're crazy about you. Believe me.

3 I feel like I've known them for a long time.

4 Dad, they don't have a shower bath (淋浴 línyù) here.

5 You need practice. Oh, shut up. Go to sleep will you?

五　自由發揮

你出去旅行的時候，喜歡住在別人家裏嗎？住在別人家有甚麼好處？
有甚麼不方便的地方？

Sure, they're crazy about you. Believe me.

3 I feel like I've known them for a long time.

4 Dad, they don't have a shower bath (淋浴 línyù) here.

5 You need practice. Oh, shut up. Go to sleep will you?

五　自由发挥

你出去旅行的时候，喜欢住在别人家裏吗？住在别人家有甚么好处？
有甚么不方便的地方？

對白

第五節 Section Five

第二十八幕到第三十五幕　Scene 28 to Scene 35

It is interesting that people in Beijing often go outside at night to sit or sing. Do people in American cities do the same? Consider the scene at the cemetary. Why is the name of this movie "A Great Wall"?

第二十八幕　---在趙家院子裏

莉莉：　　舅舅。

方先生：莉莉，還不歇着？這麼唸書，玩兒命似的，我看你。

莉莉：　　沒關係，反正睡不着。

方先生：你會粘"知了"嗎？

莉莉：　　我小時候玩兒過，不過那一般都是男孩子玩兒的。

方先生：哪兒啊？看你媽小的時候可能了。拿個大竹竿有她三個人那麼高，
　　　　往樹上一戳就是一個。他沒告訴你啊？

莉莉：　　沒有。

方先生：我們那時候住好大一所四合院兒，滿院子的螞蚱，沒事兒就逮住幾隻
　　　　螞蚱，用錫紙包上舉行"火葬"，燒出那味兒跟烤蠶豆似的，都是你
　　　　媽想出來的。不過我也發明了一個叫"水葬"-- 把螞蚱逮着，一泡
　　　　尿一滋，就把它滋死了。你老爺那時候一生氣，就坐在大樹底下唱大
　　　　鼓，難聽極了。

第二十九幕　---在方家墳地

趙太太：我們好些日子沒來了。爸爸過去的那年，正趕上亂，也沒給他好好的辦。

方先生：別說了，別說了，姐姐。

方先生：Son, come here. This is the old man I told you about. He's

52

对白

第五节 Section Five

第二十八幕到第三十五幕　Scene 28 to Scene 35

It is interesting that people in Beijing often go outside at night to sit or sing. Do people in American cities do the same? Consider the scene at the cemetary. Why is the name of this movie "A Great Wall"?

第二十八幕 ---在赵家院子里

莉莉：　舅舅。

方先生：莉莉，还不歇着？这么念书，玩儿命似的，我看你。

莉莉：　没关系，反正睡不着。

方先生：你会粘"知了"吗？

莉莉：　我小时候玩儿过，不过那一般都是男孩子玩儿的。

方先生：哪儿啊？看你妈小的时候可能了。拿个大竹竿有她三个人那么高，往树上一戳就是一个。他没告诉你啊？

莉莉：　没有。

方先生：我们那时候住好大一所四合院儿，满院子的蚂蚱，没事儿就逮住几只蚂蚱，用锡纸包上举行"火葬"，烧出那味儿跟烤蚕豆似的，都是你妈想出来的。不过我也发明了一个叫"水葬"-- 把蚂蚱逮着，一泡尿一滋，就把它滋死了。你老爷那时候一生气，就坐在大树底下唱大鼓，难听极了。

第二十九幕 ---在方家坟地

赵太太：我们好些日子没来了。爸爸过去的那年，正赶上乱，也没给他好好的办。

方先生：别说了，别说了，姐姐。

方先生：Son, come here. This is the old man I told you about. He's funnier than you and me put together. Funny man.

第三十幕 ---在時裝表演訓練班

載華： 你要他不要我呀？只有高個兒穿時裝，矮個兒就不穿了嗎？一達，走啊！

第三十一幕 ---早晨在趙家院子做運動

第三十二幕 ---在莉莉的臥房

趙太太： 莉莉，張小娟給你的信，邀你們一塊兒騎車上圓明園。學校來信要你去
　　　　 練乒乓球呢。欸，帶你表哥出去玩兒！

保羅： I can't believe this! Look at this. She reads all your mail!

莉莉： 這有甚麼啊？

保羅： Haven't you ever heard of a thing called "privacy"?

莉莉： 這有甚麼啊？

保羅： Privacy?

莉莉： Privacy.

保羅： Yeah, Alright. I guess there's no such thing in China.

第三十三幕 ---在北海業餘體校

教練： 這手不能碰檯子，一碰就算犯規，不管你打着沒打着都算你輸。
　　　　 注意點兒啊！

保羅： （手又碰檯子）

教練： 怎麼回事兒啊？剛跟你說完了，這樣，教練怎麼教你？

保羅： （點頭，表示知道了）

第三十四幕 ---在長城上

莉莉： 舅舅，你還不如我們走得快呢。小娟，快來！

funnier than you and me put together. Funny man.

第三十幕 ---在时装表演训练班

载华： 你要他不要我呀？只有高个儿穿时装，矮个儿就不穿了吗？一达，走啊！

第三十一幕 ---早晨在赵家院子做运动

第三十二幕 ---在莉莉的卧房

赵太太： 莉莉，张小娟给你的信，邀你们一块儿骑车上圆明园。学校来信要你去练乒乓球呢。欸，带你表哥出去玩儿！

保罗： I can't believe this! Look at this. She reads all your mail!

莉莉： 这有甚么啊？

保罗： Haven't you ever heard of a thing called "privacy"?

莉莉： 这有甚么啊？

保罗： Privacy?

莉莉： Privacy.

保罗： Yeah, Alright. I guess there's no such thing in China.

第三十三幕 ---在北海业余体校

教练： 这手不能碰台子，一碰就算犯规，不管你打着没打着都算你输。
注意点儿啊！

保罗： （手又碰台子）

教练： 怎么回事儿啊？刚跟你说完了，这样，教练怎么教你？

保罗： （点头，表示知道了）

第三十四幕 ---在长城上

莉莉： 舅舅，你还不如我们走得快呢。小娟，快来！

保羅： What do you think? "Put the Great Wall on your chest."

載華： "Chest" 是甚麼意思？

保羅： I'll buy it.

方先生： The Great Wall was built thousands of years ago to prevent invaders from the north.

方太太： It didn't work.

方先生： No, the invaders came from the south.

第三十五幕 ---參觀某電子研究所

總工師： <u>方</u>先生，請換上衣服。

方先生： 今兒個做大夫了。

總工師： 請換一下鞋。

方先生： 襪子有個洞。

總工師： 請您自己試試。

方先生： Ah, this character is wrong.

總工師： No, this is only simplified version.

保罗：　　What do you think? "Put the Great Wall on your chest."

载华：　　"Chest" 是甚么意思？

保罗：　　I'll buy it.

方先生：The Great Wall was built thousands of years ago to prevent invaders from the north.

方太太：It didn't work.

方先生：No, the invaders came from the south.

第三十五幕 ---参观某电子研究所

总工师：方先生，请换上衣服。

方先生：今儿个做大夫了。

总工师：请换一下鞋。

方先生：袜子有个洞。

总工师：请您自己试试。

方先生：Ah, this character is wrong.

总工师：No, this is only simplified version.

生詞及例句

第二十八幕

生詞

1	玩兒命	wán(r)mìng	to take your life into your own hands, to play with your life
2	似的	shìde	好像，similar to
3	粘	nián	to stick; sticky
*4	知了	zhīliǎo	cicada (often pronounced jiliao)
5	可能了	kě-néng-le	really quite able
*6	竹竿	zhú gān	bamboo pole
*7	戳	chuō	to stab
*8	四合院	sìhé yuàn	courtyard house
9	滿	mǎn	full
*10	螞蚱	màzha	cricket
11	逮住	dǎi zhu	to capture, to catch
12	錫紙	xī zhǐ	tinfoil
13	舉行	jǔxíng	to hold (meeting or ceremony)
14	火葬	huǒ zàng	cremation (here means burn to death)
15	燒	shāo	to burn
16	跟...似的	gēn...shìde	similar to...
17	烤	kǎo	roast
*18	蠶豆	cán dòu	dried lima beans
19	水葬	shuǐ zàng	burial at sea (here--to drown)
*20	泡	pāo	(measure word for urine)
*21	滋	zī	to squirt out

55

生词及例句

第二十八幕

生词

1	玩儿命	wán(r)mìng	to take your life into your own hands, to play with your life
2	似的	shìde	好像, similar to
3	粘	nián	to stick; sticky
*4	知了	zhīliǎo	cicada (often pronounced jiliao)
5	可能了	kě-néng-le	really quite able
*6	竹竿	zhú gān	bamboo pole
*7	戳	chuō	to stab
*8	四合院	sìhé yuàn	courtyard house
9	满	mǎn	full
*10	蚂蚱	màzha	cricket
11	逮住	dǎi zhu	to capture, to catch
12	锡纸	xī zhǐ	tinfoil
13	举行	jǔxíng	to hold (meeting or ceremony)
14	火葬	huǒ zàng	cremation (here means burn to death)
15	烧	shāo	to burn
16	跟...似的	gēn...shìde	similar to...
17	烤	kǎo	roast
*18	蚕豆	cán dòu	dried lima beans
19	水葬	shuǐ zàng	burial at sea (here--to drown)
*20	泡	pāo	(measure word for urine)
*21	滋	zī	to squirt out

*22	老爺	lǎoye	grandpa (maternal)
*23	大鼓	dàgǔ	big drum; Chinese ballad with (big) drum accompaniment, 京韻大鼓 is one school of 大鼓 where a popular story is told in song

例句

A 你不吃飯，不睡覺，就念書，這簡直是玩兒命嘛。

B 你別看他是個小孩子，他可能了，做事跟大人似的。

C 他用筆把紙戳了好幾個洞。

D 在中國滿街都是人跟自行車。

E 從前在北京的房子多半是四合院，三面有屋子，中間兒是院子。夏天晚上家裏人都在院子裏乘涼。院子裏有很多"知了"，也有"螞蚱"。"知了"在樹上叫，"螞蚱"在地上跳。小孩子喜歡用竹竿去粘"知了"，逮"螞蚱"玩兒。大人有的唱大鼓，有的唱戲，有的一邊兒喝茶，一邊兒聊天兒。很有意思。

F 他烤牛肉的時候，用錫紙包上放在火上烤，味兒很香。

G 我們打算明天給他舉行一個生日晚會。我們吃烤雞，炸蠶豆，好不好？

H 有的人死了以後希望火葬，有的人喜歡水葬，有的人喜歡土葬。你呢？

I 狗在我們院子尿了好幾泡尿。真討厭。

J 媽媽的爸爸是你的"老爺"，有的人叫"外公"，也有的人叫"外祖父"。

第二十九幕

生詞

1	過去	guòqù	to pass away; in the past; to pass through
2	正趕上	zhèng gǎnshang	right in the middle of (used when one action takes place during the

56

＊22	老爷	lǎoye	grandpa (maternal)
＊23	大鼓	dàgǔ	big drum; Chinese ballad with (big) drum accompaniment, 京韵大鼓 is one school of 大鼓 where a popular story is told in song

例句

A　你不吃饭，不睡觉，就念书，这简直是玩儿命嘛。

B　你别看他是个小孩子，他可能了，做事跟大人似的。

C　他用笔把纸戳了好几个洞。

D　在中国满街都是人跟自行车。

E　从前在北京的房子多半是四合院，三面有屋子，中间儿是院子。夏天晚上家裏人都在院子裏乘凉。院子裏有很多"知了"，也有"蚂蚱"。"知了"在树上叫，"蚂蚱"在地上跳。小孩子喜欢用竹竿去粘"知了"，逮"蚂蚱"玩儿。大人有的唱大鼓，有的唱戏，有的一边儿喝茶，一边儿聊天儿。很有意思。

F　他烤牛肉的时候，用锡纸包上放在火上烤，味儿很香。

G　我们打算明天给他举行一个生日晚会。我们吃烤鸡，炸蚕豆，好不好？

H　有的人死了以后希望火葬，有的人喜欢水葬，有的人喜欢土葬。你呢？

I　狗在我们院子尿了好几泡尿。真讨厌。

J　妈妈的爸爸是你的"老爷"，有的人叫"外公"，也有的人叫"外祖父"。

第二十九幕

生词

1	过去	guòqù	to pass away; in the past; to pass through
2	正赶上	zhèng gǎnshang	right in the middle of (used when one action takes place during the

		process of another action)
3	亂 luàn	chaotic
4	傷心 shāngxīn	to feel sad, hurt, sorrowful

例句

A "過去"有好幾個意思；在這兒是"死"的意思。別的意思是甚麼，你還記得嗎？

記得。我們可以説他過去住在中國，還可以説對不起請讓我過去。

很好。

B 我昨天到他家去的時候正趕上他們吃飯，所以我就在那兒吃了。

C 現在中國很亂，所以我的心也很亂。

D "別傷心"是"別難過"的意思。

第三十幕

生詞

1	時裝 shízhuāng	clothing, fashion

例句

A 現在的時裝多半是爲了高個兒、瘦的人穿的，矮個兒、胖的人穿着不好看。

B 中國現在也有時裝表演了？

可不是嗎，所以載華，一達到時裝表演訓練班去找工作啊！

第三十二幕

生詞

			process of another action)
3	乱	luàn	chaotic
4	伤心	shāngxīn	to feel sad, hurt, sorrowful

例句

A "过去"有好几个意思；在这儿是"死"的意思。别的意思是甚么，
你还记得吗？
记得。我们可以说他过去住在中国，还可以说对不起请让我过去。
很好。

B 我昨天到他家去的时候正赶上他们吃饭，所以我就在那儿吃了。

C 现在中国很乱，所以我的心也很乱。

D "别伤心"是"别难过"的意思。

第三十幕

生词

1	时装	shízhuāng	clothing, fashion

例句

A 现在的时装多半是为了高个儿、瘦的人穿的，矮个儿、胖的人穿着
不好看。

B 中国现在也有时装表演了？
可不是吗，所以载华，一达到时装表演训练班去找工作啊！

第三十二幕

生词

1	邀	yāo	to invite, to ask
2	騎車	qí chē	to ride a bicycle
3	表哥	biǎogē	cousin (older male)

例句

A 一達邀莉莉到公園去談談。

B 我們是騎車去還是騎馬去？

　　騎車去吧，快一點兒。

C 保羅是莉莉的表哥，莉莉是保羅的表妹。

第三十三幕

生詞

1	檯子	táizi	platform, table
2	算	suàn	to be counted as, to count
3	犯規	fàn guī	to break the rules
4	不管...都	bùguǎn...dōu	no matter what...all
5	打着	dǎzháo	to have hit
6	輸	shū	to lose (a game)
7	怎麼回事兒？	zěnme huíshì(r)	what happened? what's going on?
8	這樣	zhèi yàng	in this way

例句

A 教練告訴保羅打球的時候，手不可以碰乒乓球的檯子。可是保羅忘了，他又碰檯子了，教練就很生氣地說：「這是怎麼回事兒啊？」最後保羅賽球輸了就是因爲他的手碰了檯子犯規了。

B 這次我沒打着球，不算。

　　好，這樣吧，這次不算，下次要是你沒打着球，就算你輸了。

1	邀	yāo	to invite, to ask
2	骑车	qí chē	to ride a bicycle
3	表哥	biǎogē	cousin (older male)

例句

A 一达邀莉莉到公园去谈谈。

B 我们是骑车去还是骑马去？

骑车去吧，快一点儿。

C 保罗是莉莉的表哥，莉莉是保罗的表妹。

第三十三幕

生词

1	台子	táizi	platform, table
2	算	suàn	to be counted as, to count
3	犯规	fàn guī	to break the rules
4	不管... 都	bùguǎn...dōu	no matter what...all
5	打着	dǎzháo	to have hit
6	输	shū	to lose (a game)
7	怎么回事儿？	zěnme huíshì(r)	what happened? what's going on?
8	这样	zhèi yàng	in this way

例句

A 教练告诉保罗打球的时候，手不可以碰乒乓球的台子。可是保罗忘了，他又碰台子了，教练就很生气地说：「这是怎么回事儿啊？」最后保罗赛球输了就是因为他的手碰了台子犯规了。

B 这次我没打着球，不算。

好，这样吧，这次不算，下次要是你没打着球，就算你输了。

第三十四幕

生詞

1   還不如   hái bùrú   (still) not as good as

例句

A   你學了三年中國話了，怎麼説得還不如他呢？他才學了三個月。
     那還不簡單，他比我聰明嘛！

B   坐公共汽車還不如騎自行車去快呢。

第三十五幕

生詞

1   換   huàn   to change, exchange
2   鞋   xié   shoes
3   襪子   wàzi   socks
4   洞   dòng   hole

例句

今天莉莉的男朋友邀她出去玩兒，她換上了一件很漂亮的衣裳，她要穿高跟鞋，可是她的襪子有一個洞，不能穿了，最後她只好穿涼鞋去。穿涼鞋不必穿襪子。

第三十四幕

生词

1   还不如   hái bùrú   (still) not as good as

例句

A   你学了三年<u>中国</u>话了，怎么说得<u>还不如</u>他呢？他才学了三个月。
     那还不简单，他比我聪明嘛！
B   <u>坐公共汽车</u>还不如骑自行车去快呢。

第三十五幕

生词

1   换   huàn   to change, exchange
2   鞋   xié   shoes
3   袜子   wàzi   socks
4   洞   dòng   hole

例句

今天<u>莉莉</u>的男朋友邀她出去玩儿，她<u>换</u>上了一件很漂亮的衣裳，她要穿
高跟鞋，可是她的<u>袜子</u>有一个<u>洞</u>，不能穿了，最后她只好穿凉<u>鞋</u>去。穿
凉鞋不必穿袜子。

練習五

一　課堂討論

1　方先生跟莉莉晚上睡不着，他們在院子裏談甚麼？

2　電影兒裏為甚麼要有去墳墓 fénmù (graveyard) 的一幕？中國人到墳地去多半是帶吃的東西，美國呢？

3　一達，載華到澡堂跟到時裝表演訓練班去是要說明些甚麼？

4　早晨趙先生跟方先生都在院子裏做運動是要說明甚麼？

5　保羅跟莉莉對趙太太拆信的事，看法相同嗎？為甚麼？

6　方先生到某電子研究院參觀的時候，有甚麼事你覺得很奇怪？為甚麼？

二　問答題

1　為甚麼方先生説莉莉是"玩命似的"？

2　方先生跟他姐姐小時候調皮不調皮？他們做甚麼事讓你覺得他們很調皮？

3　在墳地 féndì (graveyard) 的時候，趙太太為甚麼很傷心？方先生在墳地跟保羅説甚麼？

4　趙太太看見方先生跟他太太擁抱 yōngbào (embrace) 的時候，為甚麼把莉莉拉開不讓她看？

5　一達跟載華到時裝表演訓練班去做甚麼？為甚麼載華沒考上？

6　為甚麼方先生不做美國的運動了，要學趙先生打太極拳 tàijí guán (Chinese shadow boxing)？

练习五

第二十八幕到第三十五幕

一 课堂讨论

1　方先生跟莉莉晚上睡不着，他们在院子裏谈甚么？

2　电影儿裏为甚么要有去坟墓 fénmù（graveyard）的一幕？中国人到坟地去多半是带吃的东西，美国呢？

3　一达，载华到澡堂跟到时装表演训练班去是要说明些甚么？

4　早晨赵先生跟方先生都在院子裏做运动是要说明甚么？

5　保罗跟莉莉对赵太太拆信的事，看法相同吗？为甚么？

6　方先生到某电子研究院参观的时候，有甚么事你觉得很奇怪？为甚么？

二 问答题

1　为甚么方先生说莉莉是"玩命似的"？

2　方先生跟他姐姐小时候调皮不调皮？他们做甚么事让你觉得他们很调皮？

3　在坟地 féndì（graveyard）的时候，赵太太为甚么很伤心？方先生在坟地跟保罗说甚么？

4　赵太太看见方先生跟他太太拥抱 yōngbào（embrace）的时候，为甚么把莉莉拉开不让她看？

5　一达跟载华到时装表演训练班去做甚么？为甚么载华没考上？

6　为甚么方先生不做美国的运动了，要学赵先生打太极拳 tàijí quán（Chinese shadow boxing）？

60

7　方太太怎麼知道<u>小娟</u>給<u>莉莉</u>的信上說甚麼？<u>方</u>太太拆看<u>莉莉</u>的信，爲
甚麼<u>保羅</u>覺得很生氣？<u>莉莉</u>爲甚麼覺得沒有甚麼？

8　在<u>北海業餘體校</u>教練告訴<u>保羅</u>打球的時候，應該注意甚麼？

9　<u>方</u>先生說<u>中國</u>的長城是甚麼時候建的？爲甚麼要建長城？

10　<u>方</u>先生爲甚麼說電腦上那個字錯了？他爲甚麼不認識簡體字？

三　造句

1　舉行

2　跟...似的：

3　正趕上：

4　邀：

5　算：

6　犯規：

7　不管...都：

8　怎麼回事兒？

9　還不如：

7　方太太怎么知道小娟给莉莉的信上说甚么？方太太拆看莉莉的信，为甚么保罗觉得很生气？莉莉为甚么觉得没有甚么？

8　在北海业余体校教练告诉保罗打球的时候，应该注意甚么？

9　方先生说中国的长城是甚么时候建的？为甚么要建长城？

10　方先生为甚么说电脑上那个字错了？他为甚么不认识简体字？

三　造句

1　举行

2　跟...似的：

3　正赶上：

4　邀：

5　算：

6　犯规：

7　不管...都：

8　怎么回事儿？

9　还不如：

10 換:

四 翻譯

1 Son, come here. This is the old man I told you about. He's
   funnier (有風趣 yǒu fēngqù) than you and me put together.

2 I can't believe this! Look at this. She reads all your mail!

3 Yeah, alright. I guess there's no such thing in China.

4 The Great Wall was built thousands of years ago to prevent
   (防止 fángzhǐ) invaders (侵略者 qīnlüè zhě) from the north.

5 Ah, this character is wrong.
   No, this only simplified version.

五 自由發揮

看了這幾幕，你對中國的風俗習慣有甚麼進一步的瞭解？

10 换：

1 Son, come here. This is the old man I told you about. He's
   funnier (有风趣 yǒu fēngqù) than you and me put together.

2 I can't believe this! Look at this. She reads all your mail!

3 Yeah, alright. I guess there's no such thing in China.

4 The Great Wall was built thousands of years ago to prevent
   (防止 fángzhǐ) invaders (侵略者 qīnlüè zhě) from the north.

5 Ah, this character is wrong.
   No, this only simplified version.

五 自由发挥

看了这几幕，你对中国的风俗习惯有甚么进一步的了解？

對白
第六節 Section Six
第三十六幕到第三十七幕　Scene 36 to Scene 37

　　In these two scenes, pay attention to how the two couples get to know each other. What is diplomatic about their behavior? Do Mr. Zhao and Grace begin to sharpen their images of the other culture?

第三十六幕 ---晚上在趙家聊天兒

趙先生：這幾十年你成天盡說外國話，那嘴巴不累得慌嗎？

方先生：久了也就習慣了，不覺得了。

方太太：He speaks Chinese all the time, with his relatives and his friends in the States.

趙太太：小弟，你們在那兒一個月掙多少錢？

趙先生：你看你，問這個，人家美國不興問這個。

趙太太：你又知道了，逞甚麼能啊，這問自己的親弟弟有甚麼不行的呢。

方太太：He earns zero dollars now.

方先生：在美國啊，掙多少錢都一樣，反正不够花的，在那兒講究誰欠錢多，誰就有本事。

趙太太：哟，那千萬別學這壞毛病。爹不是常說嗎，咱們不能靠借債過日子啊。

趙先生：你現在是跟那個單位啊？

方先生：我現在沒單位。

趙太太：人家那兒不興說單位。你那家公司叫甚麼來着？

方先生：公司也沒了。臨來的時候跟老板鬧翻了。我現在是個大閑人。待業中年，照你們這兒的話說。

趙太太：真的嗎？都這麼大歲數了，還要脾氣，那怎麼得了？找人說說，千萬別跟領導鬧意見，聽見了沒有？

方先生：來不及了。臨走的時候跟老板大吵一架，然後我把一杯熱咖啡倒在他

对白
第六节 Section Six

第三十六幕到第三十七幕　Scene 36 to Scene 37

In these two scenes, pay attention to how the two couples get to know each other. What is diplomatic about their behavior? Do Mr. Zhao and Grace begin to sharpen their images of the other culture?

第三十六幕 ---晚上在赵家聊天儿

赵先生：这几十年你成天尽说外国话，那嘴巴不累得慌吗？

方先生：久了也就习惯了，不觉得了。

方太太：He speaks Chinese all the time, with his relatives and his friends in the States.

赵太太：小弟，你们在那儿一个月挣多少钱？

赵先生：你看你，问这个，人家美国不兴问这个。

赵太太：你又知道了，逞甚么能啊，这问自己的亲弟弟有甚么不行的呢。

方太太：He earns zero dollars now.

方先生：在美国啊，挣多少钱都一样，反正不够花的，在那儿讲究谁欠钱多，谁就有本事。

赵太太：哟，那千万别学这坏毛病。爹不是常说吗，咱们不能靠借债过日子啊。

赵先生：你现在是跟那个单位啊？

方先生：我现在没单位。

赵太太：人家那儿不兴说单位。你那家公司叫甚么来着？

方先生：公司也没了。临来的时候跟老板闹翻了。我现在是个大闲人。待业中年，照你们这儿的话说。

赵太太：真的吗？都这么大岁数了，还要脾气，那怎么得了？找人说说，千万别跟领导闹意见，听见了没有？

方先生：来不及了。临走的时候跟老板大吵一架，然后我把一杯热咖啡倒在他褲子上了。

方太太：That was a cup of hot coffee, very hot.

趙太太：怎麼得了哇！這麼大歲數了，還沒個正經。

趙先生：聽說這美國差不多每個人都得性病，是真的？

方先生：Hee, hee, ha, herpes maybe!

方太太：Leo! What are you talking about?

第三十七幕 --- 在趙家

趙太太：你看這布多漂亮。來試試。

方太太：Oh, Chinese fabrics are so beautiful. Too bad they don't pay more attention to fashion.

趙太太：這個呀，做上衣服最漂亮了。來，來，挑個樣子。這個不好。太短。

方太太：Too short.

趙太太：這個衣服合適，旗袍。拿這個布啊，做旗袍最漂亮。好多人都這麼做的。

方太太：Don't you think it's too long? Too long?

趙太太：哦，不長，這旗袍就要這麼長，短到這兒就不好看了。我這就去做去，啊。

方太太：I don't think I could fit into this!

趙太太：你以後裏頭還得穿衣服呢。哦，弟妹的腰真够秀氣的。

方太太：I am too old for a maternity dress!

趙太太：上面這麼大，下面就得這麼寬，要不然不適襯，不好看。我心裏有數兒。好，我這會兒就給你做。

方太太：Oh, you're going to sew it.

趙太太：你看，這布縮水挺利害。我洗了，可能縮了不少。

趙太太：中國衣服啊，穿着身上就是舒服。

方太太：Oh! It's too big. I haven't been this big since I had Paul!

趙太太：多合適啊！

64

　　　　　　裤子上了。

方太太：That was a cup of hot coffee, very hot.

赵太太：怎么得了哇！这么大岁数了，还没个正经。

赵先生：听说这美国差不多每个人都得性病，是真的？

方先生：Hee, hee, ha, herpes maybe!

方太太：Leo! What are you talking about?

第三十七幕 ---在赵家

赵太太：你看这布多漂亮。来试试。

方太太：Oh, Chinese fabrics are so beautiful. Too bad they don't pay
　　　　more attention to fashion.

赵太太：这个呀，做上衣服最漂亮了。来，来，挑个样子。这个不好。太短。

方太太：Too short.

赵太太：这个衣服合适，旗袍。拿这个布啊，做旗袍最漂亮。好多人都这么做的。

方太太：Don't you think it's too long? Too long?

赵太太：哦，不长，这旗袍就要这么长，短到这儿就不好看了。我这就去做去，
　　　　啊。

方太太：I don't think I could fit into this!

赵太太：你以后裹头还得穿衣服呢。哦，弟妹的腰真够秀气的。

方太太：I am too old for a maternity dress!

赵太太：上面这么大，下面就得这么宽，要不然不适衬，不好看。我心裏有数儿。
　　　　好，我这会儿就给你做。

方太太：Oh, you're going to sew it.

赵太太：你看，这布缩水挺利害。我洗了，可能缩了不少。

赵太太：中国衣服啊，穿着身上就是舒服。

方太太：Oh! It's too big. I haven't been this big since I had Paul!

赵太太：多合适啊！

生詞及例句

第三十六幕

生詞

1	成天	chēngtiān	一天到晚，a whole day; always
2	嘴巴	zuǐba	嘴，mouth
3	累得慌	lèide huang	累得很，exhausted
4	習慣了	xíguàn le	accustomed to, used to
5	不覺得	bù juéde	don't feel
6	不興	bùxīng	inappropriate, improper
7	逞能	chěngnéng	to show off (one's talents)
8	親弟弟	qīn dìdi	one's own brother
9	講究	jiǎngjiu	to be fussy or particular about; to pay attention to
10	誰...誰就	shéi...shéi jiù	anyone who is...will...
11	欠錢	qiàn qián	to owe money
12	壞毛病	huài máobing	bad habit
13	爹	diē	Dad, father
14	靠...過日子	kào...guò rìzi	to depend upon...for a living
15	借債	jiè zhài	to borrow money, to take a loan
16	公司	gōngsī	company
17	老板	lǎobǎn	boss
18	跟...鬧翻	gēn...nàofān	to get in a fight with, to be on bad terms with
19	大閑人	dà-xián-rén	a man of leisure, someone not workin
20	照...話說	zhào...huà-shuō	in the words of, in (your) terms
21	待業	dàiyè	to wait for employment (Mainland

生词及例句

第三十六幕

生词

1	成天	chéngtiān	一天到晚，a whole day; always
2	嘴巴	zuǐba	嘴，mouth
3	累得慌	lèide huang	累得很，exhausted
4	习惯了	xíguàn le	accustomed to, used to
5	不觉得	bù juéde	don't feel
6	不兴	bùxīng	inappropriate, improper
7	逞能	chěngnéng	to show off (one's talents)
8	亲弟弟	qīn dìdi	one's own brother
9	讲究	jiǎngjiu	to be fussy or particular about; to pay attention to
10	谁... 谁就	shéi...shéi jiù	anyone who is...will...
11	欠钱	qiàn qián	to owe money
12	坏毛病	huài máobing	bad habit
13	爹	diē	Dad, father
14	靠... 过日子	kào...guò rìzi	to depend upon...for a living
15	借债	jiè zhài	to borrow money, to take a loan
16	公司	gōngsī	company
17	老板	lǎobǎn	boss
18	跟... 闹翻	gēn...nàofān	to get in a fight with, to be on bad terms with
19	大闲人	dà-xián-rén	a man of leisure, someone not working
20	照... 话说	zhào...huà-shuō	in the words of, in (your) terms
21	待业	dàiyè	to wait for employment (Mainland

65

Chinese expression for unemployed;
in Taiwan use 失業）

22	中年	zhōng nián	middle age
23	歲數	suìshu	age
24	耍脾氣	shuǎ píqi	to lose one's temper, lose one's cool
25	怎麼得了?	zěnme-dé-liǎo?	what are we going to do with you? this is one hell of a mess
26	說說	shuōshuō	to mediate, to put in a good word for you
27	千萬	qiānwàn	by all means
28	領導	lǐngdǎo	leader; to lead
29	鬧意見	nào yìjian	to argue; to be on bad terms because of a disagreement
*30	大吵一架	dà-chǎo-yí-jià	to have a big fight
31	倒在	dào zai	to pour on
32	褲子	kùzi	pants, trousers
33	沒個正經	méi-ge-zhèngjīng	always fooling around, doesn't take things seriously
34	性病	xìng bìng	venereal disease

例句

A "成天"是"一天到晚"的意思。比方說：他成天就知道玩兒不知道
念書，怎麼得了啊？

B 你成天罵人嘴吧不累得慌嗎？
不累，習慣了。

C 中國人覺得美國人不興問別人掙多少錢、多大歲數很奇怪。
美國人也覺得中國人一認識就問這些問題，很奇怪。
這就是中美兩國風俗習慣（social custom）不同，很有意思的地方啊！

D 因為你是我的親弟弟我才告訴你。你不能在領導面前逞能，想你甚
麼都會。

22	中年	zhōng nián	middle age
23	岁数	suìshu	age
24	耍脾气	shuǎ píqi	to lose one's temper, lose one's cool
25	怎么得了？	zěnme-dé-liǎo?	what are we going to do with you? this is one hell of a mess
26	说说	shuōshuō	to mediate, to put in a good word for you
27	千万	qiānwàn	by all means
28	领导	lǐngdǎo	leader; to lead
29	闹意见	nào yìjian	to argue; to be on bad terms because of a disagreement
*30	大吵一架	dà-chǎo-yí-jià	to have a big fight
31	倒在	dào zai	to pour on
32	裤子	kùzi	pants, trousers
33	没个正经	méi-ge-zhèngjǐng	always fooling around, doesn't take things seriously
34	性病	xìng bìng	venereal disease

例句

A "成天"是"一天到晚"的意思。比方说：他成天就知道玩儿不知道
　念书，怎么得了啊？

B 你成天骂人嘴吧不累得慌吗？
　不累，习惯了。

C 中国人觉得美国人不兴问别人挣多少钱、多大岁数很奇怪。
　美国人也觉得中国人一认识就问这些问题，很奇怪。
　这就是中美两国风俗习惯（social custom）不同，很有意思的地方啊！

D 因为你是我的亲弟弟我才告诉你。你不能在领导面前逞能，想你甚
　么都会。

E 中國人從前很講究禮貌，爲甚麼現在很多年輕人都那麼沒禮貌呢？

F 我跟我男朋友鬧翻了。我們不說話了。

  爲甚麼？

  他太講究吃。他老說我做的飯不好吃。

G 誰用功誰就考得好。

H 我沒有工作了，現在一天到晚沒事做，是個大閒人。

I 以前有工作，現在沒有了，在台灣叫失業，在大陸叫待業。

J 你到底欠他多少錢？

  誰說我欠他錢？我一分錢也不欠他的。

K 他的壞毛病很多：抽煙、喝酒，不愛做事。現在他爹死了，家裏沒
  錢了就只好靠借債過日子。

  靠借債過日子怎麼成呢！他應該找人去跟公司的老板說說，給他一
  個工作。

  誰會給他工作啊！他不但歲數大，而且還沒正經，常勾搭女人。

  又愛耍脾氣，跟別人鬧意見，吵架。

L 唉！

M 趙先生怎麼知道美國人對性關係很隨便，有性病的人不少？

N 今天我可捅了一個大婁子。我給客人倒酒的時候一不小心把一杯紅
  葡萄酒倒在客人的白褲子上了。

第三十七幕

生詞

1	漂亮	piàoliang	beautiful, pretty
2	挑	tiāo	to choose, to pick out
3	樣子	yàngzi	style; pattern
4	合適	héshì	suitable, appropriate
5	旗袍	qípáo	a formal Chinese dress (originally from the 旗人 of Manchuria)
6	這就	zhèijiù	馬上，immediately

E 中国人从前很讲究礼貌，为甚么现在很多年轻人都那么没礼貌呢？

F 我跟我男朋友闹翻了。我们不说话了。

为甚么？

他太讲究吃。他老说我做的饭不好吃。

G 谁用功谁就考得好。

H 我没有工作了，现在一天到晚没事做，是个大闲人。

I 以前有工作，现在没有了，在台湾叫失业，在大陆叫待业。

J 你到底欠他多少钱？

谁说我欠他钱？我一分钱也不欠他的。

K 他的坏毛病很多：抽烟、喝酒，不爱做事。现在他爹死了，家裏没钱了就只好靠借债过日子。

靠借债过日子怎么成呢！他应该找人去跟公司的老板说说，给他一个工作。

谁会给他工作啊！他不但岁数大，而且还没正经，常勾搭女人。

又爱耍脾气，跟别人闹意见，吵架。

L 唉！

M 赵先生怎么知道美国人对性关系很随便，有性病的人不少？

N 今天我可捅了一个大娄子。我给客人倒酒的时候一不小心把一杯红葡萄酒倒在客人的白裤子上了。

第三十七幕

生词

1	漂亮	piàoliang	beautiful, pretty
2	挑	tiāo	to choose, to pick out
3	样子	yàngzi	style; pattern
4	合适	héshì	suitable, appropriate
5	旗袍	qípáo	a formal Chinese dress (originally from the 旗人 of Manchuria)
6	这就	zhèijiù	马上，immediately

67

7	弟妹	dìmèi	sister-in-law
8	腰	yāo	waist
9	秀氣	xiùqi	thin and elegant (complimentary reference to a woman)
10	寬	kuān	wide
11	要不然	yàoburán	otherwise
12	適襯	shìchèn	fitting, suitable
13	心裏有數兒	xīn-li-yǒu-shù(r)	to know in one's heart, to have a good idea of
14	縮水	suōshuǐ	to shrink (in water)
15	厲害	lìhai	quite a lot, much, very; severe
16	舒服	shūfu	comfortable

例句

A 這雙鞋的樣子很漂亮，你挑的不錯。

B 這件旗袍我穿着不適襯，上面太小，下面太寬。

C "弟妹"是弟弟的太太。

D 她的臉長得很秀氣，可惜腰太粗不够秀氣。

E 這件衣服怎麼小了？

　大概是洗了以後縮水了。

　怎麼縮得這麼利害？現在穿着不合適了。

F 你今天不舒服，最好不要做事了。

　我心裏有數兒，不會太累的，我這就去休息。

7	弟妹	dìmèi	sister-in-law
8	腰	yāo	waist
9	秀气	xiùqi	thin and elegant (complimentary reference to a woman)
10	宽	kuān	wide
11	要不然	yàoburán	otherwise
12	适衬	shìchèn	fitting, suitable
13	心裏有数儿	xīn-li-yǒu-shù(r)	to know in one's heart, to have a good idea of
14	缩水	suōshuǐ	to shrink (in water)
15	厉害	lìhai	quite a lot, much, very; severe
16	舒服	shūfu	comfortable

例句

A 这双鞋的样子很漂亮，你挑的不错。

B 这件旗袍我穿着不适衬，上面太小，下面太宽。

C "弟妹"是弟弟的太太。

D 她的脸长得很秀气，可惜腰太粗不够秀气。

E 这件衣服怎么小了？

　　大概是洗了以后缩水了。

　　怎么缩得这么利害？现在穿着不合适了。

F 你今天不舒服，最好不要做事了。

　　我心裏有数儿，不会太累的，我这就去休息。

68

練習六

一　課堂討論

1　從第三十六幕我們可以看到中國人在夏天的晚上很喜歡坐在院子裏
　　乘涼 chéngliáng (stay cool)。
　　那天晚上都有甚麼人在那兒？桌子上放了些甚麼東西？他們談到很多
　　有意思的問題，請你說一說：
　　　　(1)　趙先生跟趙太太對美國的風俗習慣有甚麼了解？
　　　　(2)　趙先生對美國甚麼問題有興趣？
　　　　(3)　趙太太跟方先生雖然是姐弟，可是他們對領導的看法，
　　　　　　對錢的看法一樣嗎？爲甚麼？
2　你覺得趙太太對趙先生的態度 tàidu (attitude) 怎麼樣？
3　從第三十七幕，請你說說中美兩國女人對時裝有甚麼不同的看法？
　　也請你說說中國人跟美國人對親戚 qīnqi (relatives) 的態度有甚麼
　　不同？比方說如果趙太太是美國人你想她會給她第一次見面的弟妹做衣
　　服嗎？她會告訴方太太穿甚麼衣服好看嗎？
4　其他？

二　問答題

1　在美國興不興問別人掙多少錢？爲甚麼？

2　趙太太爲甚麼說趙先生逞能？趙太太對她先生客氣嗎？

3　爲甚麼方先生說在美國掙多少錢都一樣？

69

练习六

一 课堂讨论

1 从第三十六幕我们可以看到中国人在夏天的晚上很喜欢坐在院子裏
乘凉 chéngliáng (stay cool)。
那天晚上都有甚么人在那儿？桌子上放了些甚么东西？他们谈到很多
有意思的问题，请你说一说：
    (1)   赵先生跟赵太太对美国的风俗习惯有甚么了解？
    (2)   赵先生对美国甚么问题有兴趣？
    (3)   赵太太跟方先生虽然是姐弟，可是他们对领导的看法，
            对钱的看法一样吗？为甚么？
2 你觉得赵太太对赵先生的态度 tàidu (attitude) 怎么样？
3 从第三十七幕，请你说说中美两国女人对时装有甚么不同的看法？
也请你说说中国人跟美国人对亲戚 qīnqi (relatives) 的态度有甚么
不同？比方说如果赵太太是美国人你想她会给她第一次见面的弟妹做衣
服吗？她会告诉方太太穿甚么衣服好看吗？
4 其他？

二 问答题

1 在美国兴不兴问别人挣多少钱？为甚么？

2 赵太太为甚么说赵先生逞能？赵太太对她先生客气吗？

3 为甚么方先生说在美国挣多少钱都一样？

69

4 方先生說在美國"誰欠錢多誰就有本事"，爲甚麼？

5 爲甚麼趙太太說"欠錢"是壞毛病？

6 你想爲甚麼趙先生說"美國每個人都得性病"？這是真的嗎？

7 趙太太要給她弟妹做甚麼？

8 爲甚麼方太太想那衣服好像給懷孕 huáiyùn (pregnant) 的人穿的？

9 爲甚麼趙太太在做衣服以前要先把布洗一洗？

10 方太太想那件衣服合適嗎？趙太太呢？

三 造句

1 習慣：

2 覺得：

3 講究：

4 誰...誰就：

5 靠...過日子：

6 千萬：

7 鬧意見：

4　方先生说在美国"谁欠钱多谁就有本事"，为甚么？

5　为甚么赵太太说"欠钱"是坏毛病？

6　你想为甚么赵先生说"美国每个人都得性病"？这是真的吗？

7　赵太太要给她弟妹做甚么？

8　为甚么方太太想那衣服好像给怀孕 huáiyùn (pregnant) 的人穿的？

9　为甚么赵太太在做衣服以前要先把布洗一洗？

10　方太太想那件衣服合适吗？赵太太呢？

三　造句

1　习惯：

2　觉得：

3　讲究：

4　谁...谁就：

5　靠...过日子：

6　千万：

7　闹意见：

8 挑：

9 要不然：

10 利害：

四 翻譯

1 He speaks Chinese all the time, with his relatives and friends in the States.

2 Oh, Chinese fabrics are so beautiful. Too bad they don't pay more attention to fashion (式樣 shìyàng).

3 I don't think I could fit into this!

4 Oh! It's too big. I haven't been this big since I had Paul!

五 自由發揮

請你寫一個你小時候調皮或有意思的事情。

71

8 挑:

9 要不然:

10 利害:

四 翻译

1 He speaks Chinese all the time, with his relatives and
  friends in the States.

2 Oh, Chinese fabrics are so beautiful. Too bad they don't
  pay more attention to fashion (式样 shìyàng).

3 I don't think I could fit into this!

4 Oh! It's too big. I haven't been this big since I had
  Paul!

五 自由发挥

请你写一个你小时候调皮或有意思的事情。

對白

第七節 Section Seven

第三十八幕到第四十幕 Scene 38 to Scene 40

Scenes thirty-eight through forty show how the visitors add spice, and tension, to their relatives' lives. Notice Mrs. Zhao's reaction when her daughter calls her. Also, what do you notice about the scene at the dance? Why is Yida angry? Compare the father-son relationship of the Lius with that of the Fangs.

第三十八幕 ---在趙太太臥房化裝

趙太太：唉，老了。我年輕的時候啊，小的時候呀，有個小伙子，帶着小鬍子，還經常挎着。

方太太：Oh, you had a lot of guys.

趙太太：我沒嫁，嫁給這個老頭兒，又矮，又胖，肚子又大，禿腦門兒，沒事兒還（用手比着）喝酒，最討厭了。

方太太：Leo, 小弟弟。Weekend. He watches TV all weekend. He watches football.

趙太太：TV, football.

方太太：Go！Go！Doesn't pay any attention to me.

趙太太：球迷。都一樣。這老頭兒，一打開電視，就...。

莉莉： 媽。

趙太太：欸，甚麼事兒啊？

第三十九幕 ---在趙家準備去參加舞會

莉莉： Who is Linda?

72

对白
第七节 Section Seven
第三十八幕到第四十幕 Scene 38 to Scene 40

Scenes thirty-eight through forty show how the visitors add spice, and tension, to their relatives' lives. Notice Mrs. Zhao's reaction when her daughter calls her. Also, what do you notice about the scene at the dance? Why is Yida angry? Compare the father-son relationship of the Lius with that of the Fangs.

第三十八幕 ---在赵太太卧房化装

赵太太：唉，老了。我年轻的时候啊，小的时候呀，有个小伙子，带着小胡子，
还经常挎着。

方太太：Oh, you had a lot of guys.

赵太太：我没嫁，嫁给这个老头儿，又矮，又胖，肚子又大，秃脑门儿，没事儿
还（用手比着）喝酒，最讨厌了。

方太太：Leo, 小弟弟。Weekend. He watches TV all weekend. He watches
football.

赵太太：TV, football.

方太太：Go! Go! Doesn't pay any attention to me.

赵太太：球迷。都一样。这老头儿，一打开电视，就...。

莉莉：妈。

赵太太：欸，甚么事儿啊？

第三十九幕 ---在赵家准备去参加舞会

莉莉：Who is Linda?

方太太： Oh, she's just one of Paul's friends. Paul has many friends. He's very popular.

趙太太： 他們都打扮好了，我們也去搗弄，搗弄。

小娟： 這是最時興的嗎？

莉莉： 那還有錯兒。舅媽特意給我買的。

小娟： 你試試。

莉莉： 你覺得怎麼樣？

小娟： 非常漂亮。

莉莉： 這兒好像又大又鬆。

小娟： 這是給美國人穿的嘛。

一達： 小于，過來！

莉莉： 一達，一塊兒去跳舞好嗎？走吧！

趙太太： 已經晚了，快走吧！走吧！

第四十幕 --- 在劉家

劉先生： "君子固窮，小人窮斯濫矣！" 怎麼，這次準備的怎麼樣了？

一達： 還不就那麼樣。

劉先生： 這是甚麼話呢，我可提醒着你呢！你這是第三次參加高考了，要是考不上的話...

一達： 再考不上的話，我就不是人了。

劉先生： 我連督促你複習都不成了？你美的甚麼呀？你！你考不上大學還有甚麼出路？這不是明擺着的嘛！

一達： 有大學上我幹嘛不上啊！可一年就收那幾個，我有甚麼辦法。

劉先生： 收收心，抓緊時間，這次有希望。你去年不就差十二分嘛。不要搞些無聊的事情了，打乒乓，唱流行小曲兒了。

一達： 讀死書。

劉先生： 你說甚麼？你看不上你爸爸讀死書，那你又會甚麼？忘本的東西。每天做夢都想跟那趙家的閨女。清醒點兒吧，趙家和咱們不是一號人。

方太太：Oh, she's just one of Paul's friends. Paul has many friends. He's very popular.

赵太太：他们都打扮好了，我们也去捣弄，捣弄。

小娟： 这是最时兴的吗？

莉莉： 那还有错儿。舅妈特意给我买的。

小娟： 你试试。

莉莉： 你觉得怎么样？

小娟： 非常漂亮。

莉莉： 这儿好像又大又松。

小娟： 这是给美国人穿的嘛。

一达： 小于，过来！

莉莉： 一达，一块儿去跳舞好吗？走吧！

赵太太：已经晚了，快走吧！走吧！

第四十幕 ---在刘家

刘先生："君子固穷，小人穷斯滥矣！"怎么，这次准备的怎么样了？

一达： 还不就那么样。

刘先生：这是甚么话呢，我可提醒着你呢！你这是第三次参加高考了，要是考不上的话...

一达： 再考不上的话，我就不是人了。

刘先生：我连督促你复习都不成了？你美的甚么呀？你！你考不上大学还有甚么出路？这不是明摆着的嘛！

一达： 有大学上我干嘛不上啊！可一年就收那几个，我有甚么办法。

刘先生：收收心，抓紧时间，这次有希望。你去年不就差十二分嘛。不要搞些无聊的事情了，打乒乓，唱流行小曲儿了。

一达： 读死书。

刘先生：你说甚么？你看不上你爸爸读死书，那你又会甚么？忘本的东西。每天做梦都想跟那赵家的闺女。清醒点儿吧，赵家和咱们不是一号人。

73

生詞及例句

生詞

1	年輕	niánqīng	young; youth
2	小伙子	xiǎo-huǒzi	kid, teenager
3	小鬍子	xiǎo húzi	mustache
4	經常	jīngcháng	often, usually
5	挎着	kuàzhe	arm in arm, with locked arms
6	嫁	jià	to marry (for women only)
7	肚子	dùzi	stomach, belly
*8	禿腦門兒	tū nǎomén(r)	bald head
9	球迷	qiúmí	a fan of ballgames
10	打開	dǎkāi	to turn on, to open

例句

A 她最近認識了一個男孩子。那個小伙子，經常來找她。他們倆關係很不錯了。我看見他們走路的時候挎着走。也許快要結婚了。

B 趙太太為甚麼不嫁給那個留着小鬍子的年輕小伙子，要嫁給一個又矮又胖的老頭兒呢？那個老頭兒肚子大得像個鼓，而且頭髮也沒了，禿腦門兒亮得像電燈。
也許他是高幹，有錢也有地位吧？

C 他是個足球迷，一看球飯也不吃，廁所也不上，甚麼都忘了。

D 請把電視打開，就要賽球了。

第三十九幕

74

生词及例句

生词

1	年轻	niánqīng	young; youth
2	小伙子	xiǎo-huǒzi	kid, teenager
3	小胡子	xiǎo húzi	mustache
4	经常	jīngcháng	often, usually
5	挎着	kuàzhe	arm in arm, with locked arms
6	嫁	jià	to marry (for women only)
7	肚子	dùzi	stomach, belly
*8	秃脑门儿	tū nǎomén(r)	bald head
9	球迷	qiúmí	a fan of ballgames
10	打开	dǎkāi	to turn on, to open

例句

A 她最近认识了一个男孩子。那个小伙子，经常来找她。他们俩关系很不错了。我看见他们走路的时候挎着走。也许快要结婚了。

B 赵太太为甚么不嫁给那个留着小胡子的年轻小伙子，要嫁给一个又矮又胖的老头儿呢？那个老头儿肚子大得像个鼓，而且头发也没了，秃脑门儿亮得像电灯。
也许他是高干，有钱也有地位吧？

C 他是个足球迷，一看球饭也不吃，厕所也不上，甚么都忘了。

D 请把电视打开，就要赛球了。

第三十九幕

74

生詞

1	打扮	dǎban	to dress up, to make up
*2	搗弄	dǎonong	to fix up (less fussy than 打扮)
3	時興	shíxīng	fashionable, popular
4	特意	tèyì	especially
5	那還 有錯兒？	nà-hái- yǒu-cuò(r)?	一定不會錯，how can that be wrong?
6	又大又鬆	yòu dà- yòu sōng	big and loose
7	跳舞	tiàowǔ	to dance

例句

A 女孩子要去跳舞的時候都特意打扮得很漂亮。

B "搗弄"是隨便收拾收拾的意思，沒有打扮那麼正式。

C 今年最時興的衣服是甚麼樣子的？

是又大又鬆又短的樣子。去年的樣子不時興了。

誰說的？

我媽說的。她是時裝專家。還會有錯兒。

第四十幕

生詞

*1	君子固窮， 小人窮斯 濫矣！	jūnzi gù qióng xiǎorén qióng sī làn yi!	君子 (The gentleman/man of noble character) must endure hardship, but 小人 (the mean man, as opposed to real gentleman) in want, gives way to unbridled

75

生词

1	打扮	dǎban	to dress up, to make up
*2	捣弄	dǎonong	to fix up (less fussy than 打扮)
3	时兴	shíxīng	fashionable, popular
4	特意	tèyì	especially
5	那还 有错儿？	nà-hái- yǒu-cuò(r)?	一定不会错, how can that be wrong?
6	又大又松	yòu dà- yòu sōng	big and loose
7	跳舞	tiàowǔ	to dance

例句

A 女孩子要去跳舞的时候都特意打扮得很漂亮。

B "捣弄"是随便收拾收拾的意思，没有打扮那么正式。

C 今年最时兴的衣服是甚么样子的？

是又大又松又短的样子。去年的样子不时兴了。

谁说的？

我妈说的。她是时装专家。还会有错儿。

第四十幕

生词

*1	君子固穷， 小人穷斯 滥矣！	Jūnzi gù qióng xiǎorén qióng sī làn yì!	君子 (The gentleman/man of noble character) must endure hardship, but 小人 (the mean man, as opposed to real gentleman) in want, gives way to unbridled

2	還不就那麼樣？	hái-bù-jiù nàma-yàng?	nothing new, isn't it always the same?
3	提醒	tíxǐng	to remind
4	連...都	liān...dōu	even... (emphasizing an extreme)
5	督促	dūcù	to urge someone to finish a task
6	複習	fùxì	to review (one's lessons)
7	你美的甚麼呀？	nǐ-měi-de shénme-ya?	what's so great about you?
8	出路	chūlù	future, job opportunity
9	明擺着	míng-bǎi-zhe	obvious, apparent
10	收	shōu	to accept (by a school); to receive
11	收收心	shōushou-xīn	to discipline, to restrain oneself
12	抓緊	zhuājǐn	to grasp tightly (here-- to not waste)
13	差	chà	to lack, to fall short of
14	無聊	wúliáo	useless, senseless; boring; stupid
15	流行	liúxíng	popular; in vogue
16	小曲兒	xiǎo-qǔ(r)	song, ditty
17	讀死書	dú-sǐ-shū	to read old (dead) books; to read but not understand, not applying the wisdom of books
18	看不上	kàn-bu-shàng	看不起, to disrespect; 不喜歡, to not like

			license. (Confucian Analects: Book XV, Wei Ling Kung.)
2	还不就那么样？	hái-bù-jiù nàma-yàng?	nothing new, isn't it always the same?
3	提醒	tíxǐng	to remind
4	连...都	lián...dōu	even... (emphasizing an extreme)
5	督促	dūcù	to urge someone to finish a task
6	复习	fùxí	to review (one's lessons)
7	你美的甚么呀？	nǐ-měi-de shénme-ya?	what's so great about you?
8	出路	chūlù	future, job opportunity
9	明摆着	míng-bǎi-zhe	obvious, apparent
10	收	shōu	to accept (by a school); to receive
11	收收心	shōushou-xīn	to discipline, to restrain oneself
12	抓紧	zhuājǐn	to grasp tightly (here-- to not waste)
13	差	chà	to lack, to fall short of
14	无聊	wúliáo	useless, senseless; boring; stupid
15	流行	liúxíng	popular; in vogue
16	小曲儿	xiǎo-qǔ(r)	song, ditty
17	读死书	dú-sǐ-shū	to read old (dead) books; to read but not understand, not applying the wisdom of books
18	看不上	kàn-bu-shàng	看不起, to disrespect; 不喜欢, to not like

19	忘本的	wàng-běn-de	one who forgets one's
	東西	dōngxi	heritage or better past
			or bitter past
20	做夢	zuòmèng	to dream
21	清醒點兒	qīngxǐng diǎn(r)	be realistic, keep a clear
			head, "wake up and smell
			the coffee"; to come to one's
			senses
22	一號人	yí-hào-rén	people with the same
			background and social status

例句

A 你最近身體怎麼樣？

　還不就那麼樣，不好也不壞，老樣子。

B 請你提醒我，明天晚上參加莉莉的舞會。

C 老師天天督促我複習功課。

D 你為甚麼看不上住胡同的？你有甚麼了不起的？你美的甚麼呀？

E 為甚麼中學畢業要上大學呢？大學畢業以後還不是找不到事，沒有出路。

F 一達喜歡莉莉，這是明擺着的嘛！你怎麼看不出來？

G 去年我們學校收了兩千個學生。

H 快考試了，我不能再玩兒了，得收收心 、抓緊時間好好念書了。

I 你想打乒乓，唱流行小曲兒是無聊的事情嗎？

　我想不是。我想每天沒事做，做白日夢 (day dream)，或是讀死書

　才無聊呢。

J 劉先生罵一達是"忘本的東西"是因為他父親覺得他把一達養大了，

　到現在他看不起他父親了。

K 我昨天做了一個很可怕的夢。我夢見明天得參加高考。

L 他喝酒喝得太多了，現在腦子不清醒，別問他了。

M 劉先生說：「他們跟趙家不是一號人」意思是趙家是離休高幹，又

　有錢又有地位，可是他們是住大雜院兒的，又窮又沒地位，所以

19	忘本的	wàng-běn-de	one who forgets one's
	东西	dōngxi	heritage or better past
			or bitter past
20	做梦	zuòmèng	to dream
21	清醒点儿	qīngxǐng diǎn(r)	be realistic, keep a clear
			head, "wake up and smell
			the coffee"; to come to one's
			senses
22	一号人	yí-hào-rén	people with the same
			background and social status

例句

A 你最近身体怎么样？

　　还不就那么样，不好也不坏，老样子。

B 请你提醒我，明天晚上参加莉莉的舞会。

C 老师天天督促我复习功课。

D 你为甚么看不上住胡同的？你有甚么了不起的？你美的甚么呀？

E 为甚么中学毕业要上大学呢？大学毕业以后还不是找不到事，没有出路。

F 一达喜欢莉莉，这是明摆着的嘛！你怎么看不出来？

G 去年我们学校收了两千个学生。

H 快考试了，我不能再玩儿了，得收收心 、抓紧时间好好念书了。

I 你想打乒乓，唱流行小曲儿是无聊的事情吗？

　　我想不是。我想每天没事做，做白日梦（day dream），或是读死书

　　才无聊呢。

J 刘先生骂一达是"忘本的东西"是因为他父亲觉得他把一达养大了，

　　到现在他看不起他父亲了。

K 我昨天做了一个很可怕的梦。我梦见明天得参加高考。

L 他喝酒喝得太多了，现在脑子不清醒，别问他了。

M 刘先生说：「他们跟赵家不是一号人」意思是赵家是离休高干，又

　　有钱又有地位，可是他们是住大杂院儿的，又穷又没地位，所以

不是一個階層 jiēcéng (same class) 的人。

不是一个阶层 jiēcéng (same class) 的人。

練習七

一 課堂討論

1 趙太太跟方太太一邊兒打扮一邊兒談甚麼？

2 莉莉叫趙太太的時候，為甚麼趙太太把口紅 kǒuhóng (lipstick) ，
粉 fěn (face powder) 擦掉 cādiào (wipe off) ？

3 莉莉跟朋友們去參加舞會的時候為甚麼一達很生氣？

4 劉先生跟兒子為了甚麼事情鬧意見？在美國的父親也那麼罵孩子嗎？

二 問答題

1 趙太太結婚以前有甚麼樣的男朋友？

2 趙太太喜歡她的先生嗎？你怎麼知道？

3 為甚麼莉莉說她穿的那件衣服是最時興的？

4 莉莉打扮得那麼漂亮要去做甚麼？

5 劉先生為甚麼要提醒一達得收收心，抓緊時間念書？

6 一達去年差多少分沒考上大學？

7 劉先生說一達成天都做些甚麼無聊的事？

练习七

一 课堂讨论

1 赵太太跟方太太一边儿打扮一边儿谈甚么？

2 莉莉叫赵太太的时候，为甚么赵太太把口红 kǒuhóng（lipstick），
   粉 fěn（face powder） 擦掉 cādiào（wipe off）？

3 莉莉跟朋友们去参加舞会的时候为甚么一达很生气？

4 刘先生跟儿子为了甚么事情闹意见？在美国的父亲也那么骂孩子吗？

二 问答题

1 赵太太结婚以前有甚么样的男朋友？

2 赵太太喜欢她的先生吗？你怎么知道？

3 为甚么莉莉说她穿的那件衣服是最时兴的？

4 莉莉打扮得那么漂亮要去做甚么？

5 刘先生为甚么要提醒一达得收收心，抓紧时间念书？

6 一达去年差多少分没考上大学？

7 刘先生说一达成天都做些甚么无聊的事？

8 你想一達是一個不用功的孩子嗎？爲甚麽？

9 爲甚麽劉先生不願意一達跟莉莉做朋友？

10 爲甚麽劉先生罵一達是“忘本的東西”？

三 造句

1 年輕：

2 經常：

3 打開：

4 打扮：

5 又...又：

6 提醒：

7 連...都：

8 督促：

9 複習：

10 看不上：

四 翻譯

8　　你想<u>一达</u>是一个不用功的孩子吗？为甚么？

9　　为甚么<u>刘先生</u>不愿意<u>一达</u>跟<u>莉莉</u>做朋友？

10　　为甚么<u>刘先生</u>骂<u>一达</u>是"忘本的东西"？

三　造句

1　　年轻：

2　　经常：

3　　打开：

4　　打扮：

5　　又...又：

6　　提醒：

7　　连...都：

8　　督促：

9　　复习：

10　　看不上：

四　翻译

1   He doesn't pay any attention to me.

2   Don't you think it's too long?

3   Oh, you had a lot of guys.

4   Who is Linda?
    Oh, she's just one of Paul's friends. Paul has many friends.

五　自由發揮

　　要是你到中國去，中國人會常問你很多你個人的事情。比方説：你幾歲？
你有異性朋友沒有？你結婚了沒有？你一個月掙多少錢？你怎麼應付這
些問題？請你問問你的中國朋友，爲甚麼中國人要問一個剛認識的人這
些問題。

1 He doesn't pay any attention to me.

2 Don't you think it's too long?

3 Oh, you had a lot of guys.

4 Who is Linda?
   Oh, she's just one of Paul's friends. Paul has many friends.

五　自由发挥

　　要是你到中国去，中国人会常问你很多你个人的事情。比方说：你几岁？
你有异性朋友没有？你结婚了没有？你一个月挣多少钱？你怎么应付这
些问题？请你问问你的中国朋友，为甚么中国人要问一个刚认识的人这
些问题。

對白

第八節 Section Eight

第四十一幕到第四十六幕 Scene 41 to Scene 46

In this section, some similarities between Paul and Lili emerge. What has Paul learned about life in China? Does he adapt well? Consider the musical performance. Why do you think it is included? Luò Yùshēng, the woman who performs 大鼓 (Chinese ballad with drum accompaniment), is one of China's most famous artists in this genre. Who enjoys the show? Why?

第四十一幕 ---在莉莉的臥房

趙太太：欸，一達寄給你的信。他說呀...

莉莉：　媽，往後你別拆我的信了。

趙太太：甚麼？

莉莉：　拆看別人的信不好。

趙太太："別人"！你又不是"別人"，你是我女兒。

莉莉：　那也不好。

趙太太：怎麼？你幹了甚麼壞事了？連你媽都瞞着？

莉莉：　我沒瞞着。privacy.

趙太太：啊？甚麼呀？

莉莉：　privacy 就是 privacy，舅舅說不能翻譯。

趙太太：長翅膀了。現在盡拿洋文兒來曚我。你也不想想，沒有你媽媽，哪兒來的你！哼！

第四十二幕 ---北京早上的公園

对白

第八节 Section Eight

第四十一幕到第四十六幕 Scene 41 to Scene 46

In this section, some similarities between Paul and Lili emerge. What has Paul learned about life in China? Does he adapt well? Consider the musical performance. Why do you think it is included? Luò Yùshēng, the woman who performs 大鼓 (Chinese ballad with drum accompaniment), is one of China's most famous artists in this genre. Who enjoys the show? Why?

第四十一幕 ---在莉莉的卧房

赵太太：欸，一达寄给你的信。他说呀...

莉莉：　妈，往后你别拆我的信了。

赵太太：甚么？

莉莉：　拆看别人的信不好。

赵太太："别人"！你又不是"别人"，你是我女儿。

莉莉：　那也不好。

赵太太：怎么？你干了甚么坏事了？连你妈都瞒着？

莉莉：　我没瞒着。privacy.

赵太太：啊？甚么呀？

莉莉：　privacy 就是 privacy，舅舅说不能翻译。

赵太太：长翅膀了。现在尽拿洋文儿来蒙我。你也不想想，没有你妈妈，哪儿来的你！哼！

第四十二幕 ---北京早上的公园

82

第四十三幕 ---保羅，莉莉趕公共汽車

第四十四幕--- 趙先生，方先生在飯館兒

趙先生：味道怎麼樣？

方先生：够酸的。

保羅：　Dad...money...

方先生：Running out again?

趙先生：您那位今姐啊，樣樣都好，就是愛疵瞪人，當着孩子面兒、客人面兒也疵瞪，一點兒面子也不給。欸，你們那位怎麼樣？

方先生：一樣。古今中外都一樣。

趙先生：他們説，這女人到了更年期，這話很難説，醋勁兒特別大。唉，都這麼大歲數了，還能怎麼樣呢？真是。

方先生：那也説不定啊！噢，menopause 在外國也有這種説法。這女人一進了menopause 特別來勁兒。很難纏啊，活動能力很強，sexually very active　不過我沒經驗。我這是聽人説的。

趙先生：是啊！

方先生：哪兒屋兒？北屋兒。

趙先生：來，來，上北屋。哪是北屋啊？這邊兒是北屋。

方先生：走，走，上北房，上北房。

趙先生：哪兒是北啊？這邊兒。你啊，喝醉了。

方先生：沒醉。

趙先生：這是北屋。

方先生：Ah, music!

趙先生：試試，這個最靈了。

方先生：噯，不，不。

趙先生：你要是醉了啊，...

方先生：沒醉。

趙先生：你醉了就掏不成耳朵。這點兒足有半斤。看你的。

方先生：沒問題。

83

第四十三幕 ---保罗，莉莉赶公共汽车

第四十四幕--- 赵先生，方先生在饭馆儿

赵先生：味道怎么样？

方先生：够酸的。

保　罗：Dad...money...

方先生：Running out again?

赵先生：您那位令姐啊，样样都好，就是爱疵瞪人，当着孩子面儿、客人面儿
　　　　也疵瞪，一点儿面子也不给。欸，你们那位怎么样？

方先生：一样。古今中外都一样。

赵先生：他们说，这女人到了更年期，这话很难说，醋劲儿特别大。唉，都这
　　　　么大岁数了，还能怎么样呢？真是。

方先生：那也说不定啊！噢，menopause 在外国也有这种说法。这女人一进了
　　　　menopause 特别来劲儿。很难缠啊，活动能力很强，sexually very
　　　　active 不过我没经验。我这是听人说的。

赵先生：是啊！

方先生：哪儿屋儿？北屋儿。

赵先生：来，来，上北屋。哪是北屋啊？这边儿是北屋。

方先生：走，走，上北房，上北房。

赵先生：哪儿是北啊？这边儿。你啊，喝醉了。

方先生：没醉。

赵先生：这是北屋。

方先生：Ah，music！

赵先生：试试，这个最灵了。

方先生：嗳，不，不。

赵先生：你要是醉了啊，...

方先生：没醉。

赵先生：你醉了就掏不成耳朵。这点儿足有半斤。看你的。

方先生：没问题。

第四十五幕 ---在某曲藝表演場聽京韻大鼓

（唱詞）漢末諸侯亂紛爭，群雄四起動刀兵，曹孟德位壓群臣權勢重，挾持
天子把令行。都只爲要那劉表來歸順，要請一位風流名士前往疏通。
那孔融愛重儒生憐才子，修本上表要保薦彌衡 ...

(pinyin) Hànmò zhūhóu luàn fēn zhēng, qún xióng sì qǐ dòng dāo bīng,
Cáo Mèngdé wèi yāng qún chén quánshì zhòng, xiéchí tiānzǐ bǎ
lìng xíng. Dōu zhǐ wèi yào nà Liú Biǎo lái guīshùn, yào qǐng
yí wèi fēngliú míngshì wǎng shūtōng. Nà Kǒng Róng aìzhōng
rúshēng lián cáizǐ, xiū běn shàng biǎo yào bǎojiàn Mí Héng
...

(English) In the last days of the Han Dynasty, heroes and bandits vied
for power and land. The Premier Cáo Mèngdé (commonly called Cáo
Cao) was very powerful. He had the emperor in his power and
ordered the dukes about in his own name. In order to lure Liú
Biǎo (another regional leader) to come and pay allegiance to
Cáo, Cáo decided to use a scholar to mediate. Kǒng Róng (his
chief of the General Staff) had great respect for intellectuals
and recommended a young talented scholar named Mí Héng to Cáo
Cao... (to persuade Liú Biǎo to come over and to give allegiance
to Cáo.)

第四十六幕 ---早晨在劉家院子

莉莉：　Paul，這一句是甚麼意思？

趙先生：大清早的嚷嚷甚麼啊？唉，車也不知道擦。

保羅：　4th down, 15 to go. You're dead.

莉莉：　You want to bet?

保羅：　Yeah.

趙先生：莉莉！

莉莉：　Hey, touchdown!

第四十五幕 ---在某曲艺表演场听京韵大鼓

（唱词） 汉末诸侯乱纷争，群雄四起动刀兵，曹孟德位压群臣权势重，挟持
天子把令行。都只为要那刘表来归顺，要请一位风流名士前往疏通。
那孔融爱重儒生怜才子，修本上表要保荐弥衡 ...

(pinyin) Hànmò zhūhóu luàn fēn zhēng, qún xióng sǐ qǐ dòng dāo bīng,
Cáo Mèngdé wèi yāng qún chén quánshì zhòng, xiéchí tiānzǐ bǎ
lìng xíng. Dōu zhǐ wèi yào nà Liú Biǎo lái guìshùn, yào qǐng
yí wèi fēngliú míngshì wǎng shūtōng. Nà Kǒng Róng àizhòng
rúshēng lián cáizǐ, xiú běn shàng biǎo yào bǎojiàn Mí Héng
...

(English) In the last days of the Han Dynasty, heroes and bandits vied
for power and land. The Premier Cáo Mèngdé (commonly called Cao
Cao) was very powerful. He had the emperor in his power and
ordered the dukes about in his own name. In order to lure Liú
Biǎo (another regional leader) to come and pay allegiance to
Cáo, Cáo decided to use a scholar to mediate. Kǒng Róng (his
chief of the General Staff) had great respect for intellectuals
and recommended a young talented scholar named Mí Héng to Cáo
Cao... (to persuade Liú Biǎo to come over and to give allegiance
to Cáo.)

第四十六幕 ---早晨在刘家院子

莉莉： Paul，这一句是甚么意思？

赵先生：大清早的嚷嚷甚么啊？唉，车也不知道擦。

保罗： 4th down, 15 to go. You're dead.

莉莉： You want to bet?

保罗： Yeah.

赵先生：莉莉！

莉莉： Hey, touchdown!

保羅： Beginner's luck.

趙先生：莉莉，莉莉，你問問保羅，他那衣服是甚麼料子的？

莉莉： 幹嘛呀？人家正忙呢。

趙先生：忙？你就是忙玩兒呢。嘻，這麻布袋，這胳膊肘還補個補丁。

莉莉： Broken, there?

保羅： Oh, this? No. This is the style, this is fashion. This is the best, really. Pierre Cardin.

趙先生：這褲子也是去年的。這小伙子正竄個兒。

莉莉： 你別瞎說了。人家是條新褲子，最時興的樣子了。

趙先生：得了吧！粗布褲子。你舅舅啊，在那邊兒混得也夠嗆，困難啊！

保羅： No, you don't understand. These here, these are Calvin Kleins.

趙先生：這是我在五七幹校勞動時候穿的，有好幾條呢。這在那美國能流行吧？

莉莉： 爸爸！

保罗： Beginner's luck.

赵先生：莉莉，莉莉，你问问保罗，他那衣服是甚么料子的？

莉莉： 干嘛呀？人家正忙呢。

赵先生：忙？你就是忙玩儿呢。嗐，这麻布袋，这胳膊肘还补个补丁。

莉莉： Broken, there?

保罗： Oh, this? No. This is the style, this is fashion. This is the best, really. Pierre Cardin.

赵先生：这裤子也是去年的。这小伙子正审个儿。

莉莉： 你别瞎说了。人家是条新裤子，最时兴的样子了。

赵先生：得了吧！粗布裤子。你舅舅啊，在那边儿混得也够呛，困难啊！

保罗： No, you don't understand. These here, these are Calvin Kleins.

赵先生：这是我在五七干校劳动时候穿的，有好几条呢。这在那美国能流行吧？

莉莉： 爸爸！

生詞及例句

第四十一幕

生詞

1	往後	wàng hòu	從現在起，from now on
2	拆	chāi	to unseal; to open up; to tear down
3	瞞着	mánzhe	to keep secret, to hide from
4	翻譯	fānyì	to translate; translation
5	長翅膀了	zhǎng chìbǎngle	to grow wings, to think you can make it alone
6	拿...來矇我	ná...lái mēng wǒ	to use...to confuse me, to deceive me
7	洋文兒	yáng wén(r)	外國話，foreign language
8	哼	heng/hng ↘	(interjection of disgust, anger, or contempt)

例句

A　"往後"是"從今以後"的意思。比方説：往後我再也不拆你的信了。

B　"拆"在這兒是"打開"的意思。"拆信"是把信打開的意思。

C　要是你做了壞事，你是瞞着你父母還是告訴他們？

D　(privacy) 很難翻成中文，因為中國人沒有 (privacy) 這個概念，所以找不到合適的字來翻譯。

E　"長翅膀了"的意思是你現在"長大了，有本事了，好像小鳥兒一樣有翅膀會飛了，不需要父母的照顧 zhàogu (take care) 了，就不聽父母的話了."

生词及例句

第四十一幕

生词

1	往后	wàng hòu	从现在起，from now on
2	拆	chāi	to unseal; to open up; to tear down
3	瞒着	mánzhe	to keep secret, to hide from
4	翻译	fānyì	to translate; translation
5	长翅膀了	zhǎng chìbǎngle	to grow wings, to think you can make it alone
6	拿...来蒙我	ná...lái mēng wǒ	to use...to confuse me, to deceive me
7	洋文儿	yáng wén(r)	外国话，foreign language
8	哼	heng/hng	(interjection of disgust, anger, or contempt)

例句

A "往后"是"从今以后"的意思。比方说：往后我再也不拆你的信了。

B "拆"在这儿是"打开"的意思。"拆信"是把信打开的意思。

C 要是你做了坏事，你是瞒着你父母还是告诉他们？

D (privacy) 很难翻成中文，因为中国人没有 (privacy) 这个概念，所以找不到合适的字来翻译。

E "长翅膀了"的意思是你现在"长大了，有本事了，好像小鸟儿一样有翅膀会飞了，不需要父母的照顾 zhàogu (take care) 了，就不听父母的话了。"

F　趙太太説 "拿洋文來矇我" 是因為趙太太不懂英文，可是莉莉故意
　　gùyì (deliberately) 跟她説 "英文" 讓她聽不懂。

G　"洋文" 是 "外國文/話" 的意思。比方説：英文，俄文，日文等對
　　中國人來説，都是洋文。

第四十四幕

生詞

1	味道	wèidao	taste, smell
2	酸酸兒的	suānsuān(r)de	a bit sour
3	令姐	lìng jiě	your sister (polite)
4	疵瞪	cīdeng	to put (someone) down, to criticize
5	當... 面兒	dāng...miàn(r)	in front of (others)
6	面子	miànzi	face (abstract), reputation
7	古今中外	gǔ-jīn-zhōng-wài	everything (old-new-Chinese-foreign, for all times and for all conditions)
8	更年期	gēng-nián-qī	menopause
9	醋勁兒	cùjìng(r)	to be jealous, jealousy
10	來勁兒	láijìng(r)	to get excited; very interested
11	難纏	nán chán	難應付, difficult to deal with
12	經驗	jīngyàn	experience
13	喝醉了	hēzuìle	to be drunk, get drunk
14	靈	líng	effective
*15	掏耳朵	tāo ěrduo	to clean ears
16	足	zú	a full, a whole (emphasizing amount)
17	半斤	bàn jīn	half-pound (斤 is a Chinese pound, 一斤=1/2 kilogram)

F 赵太太说"拿洋文来蒙我"是因为赵太太不懂英文，可是莉莉故意
　　gùyì (deliberately) 跟她说"英文"让她听不懂。

6 "洋文"是"外国文／话"的意思。比方说：英文，俄文，日文等对
　　中国人来说，都是洋文。

第四十四幕

生词

1	味道	wèidao	taste, smell
2	酸酸儿的	suānsuān(r)de	a bit sour
3	令姐	lìng jiě	your sister (polite)
4	疵瞪	cīdeng	to put (someone) down, to criticize
5	当... 面儿	dāng...miàn(r)	in front of (others)
6	面子	miànzi	face (abstract), reputation
7	古今中外	gǔ-jīn-zhōng-wài	everything (old-new-Chinese-foreign, for all times and for all conditions)
8	更年期	gēng-nián-qī	menopause
9	醋劲儿	cùjìng(r)	to be jealous, jealousy
10	来劲儿	láijìng(r)	to get excited; very interested
11	难缠	nán chán	难应付, difficult to deal with
12	经验	jīngyàn	experience
13	喝醉了	hēzuìle	to be drunk, get drunk
14	灵	líng	effective
*15	掏耳朵	tāo ěrduo	to clean ears
16	足	zú	a full, a whole (emphasizing amount)
17	半斤	bàn jīn	half-pound (斤 is a Chinese pound, 一斤=1/2 kilogram)

87

例句

A 這個菜的味道怎麼樣？

不錯，<u>酸酸的</u>挺好吃的。一定放醋了吧？

B "令"是客氣話"您的"的意思。比方説："令姐"是"您的姐姐"的意思
"令弟"就是"您的弟弟"的意思。記住，不能説自己的姐姐是"令姐．"

C <u>趙</u>太太常常喜歡<u>疵瞪</u>他，讓他覺得很生氣。

D 別<u>當</u>着外人的<u>面疵瞪</u>我好不好？給我留點兒<u>面子</u>。

E "古今中外"的意思是"從古時候到現在，不論<u>中國</u>或外國"

F 如果到了<u>更年期</u>覺得不舒服，應該去看大夫。

G 他的先生<u>醋勁兒</u>可真大，一看見他太太跟別的男人説話，他就生氣。

H 他是個球迷，一説看球，他就<u>來勁兒</u>了。

I 這個孩子真<u>難纏</u>，你跟他説甚麼他都不聽。

J 你有沒有教<u>中文</u>的<u>經驗</u>？

K 要是你<u>喝醉</u>了，就最好不要開車，因爲你的腦子不<u>靈</u>了。

L 不要隨便<u>掏</u>耳朵，因爲一不小心就會把耳朵弄疼了。

M 那個人真胖，我想他足有兩百<u>斤</u>重。

第四十六幕

生詞

1	嚷嚷	rǎngrang	to shout
2	料子	liàozi	布, material, cloth
3	嗐	hàiˋ	(interjection showing minor disagreement)
*4	蔴布袋	mábù dài	burlap sack
5	胳膊肘	gēbozhǒu	elbow; sleeve around elbow
6	補	bǔ	to mend, to patch
*7	補丁	bǔding	patch
*8	竄個兒	cuāngè(r)	to grow very quickly (kids)

例句

A 这个菜的味道怎么样？

不错，酸酸的挺好吃的。一定放醋了吧？

B "令"是客气话"您的"的意思。比方说："令姐"是"您的姐姐"的意思
"令弟"就是"您的弟弟"的意思。记住，不能说自己的姐姐是"令姐．"

C 赵太太常常喜欢疵瞪他，让他觉得很生气。

D 别当着外人的面疵瞪我好不好？给我留点儿面子。

E "古今中外"的意思是"从古时候到现在，不论中国或外国"

F 如果到了更年期觉得不舒服，应该去看大夫。

G 他的先生醋劲儿可真大，一看见他太太跟别的男人说话，他就生气。

H 他是个球迷，一说看球，他就来劲儿了。

I 这个孩子真难缠，你跟他说甚么他都不听。

J 你有没有教中文的经验？

K 要是你喝醉了，就最好不要开车，因为你的脑子不灵了。

L 不要随便掏耳朵，因为一不小心就会把耳朵弄疼了。

M 那个人真胖，我想他足有两百斤重。

第四十六幕

生词

1	嚷嚷	rāngrang	to shout
2	料子	liàozi	布, material, cloth
3	嗐	hai ↘	(interjection showing minor disagreement)
*4	麻布袋	mábù dài	burlap sack
5	胳膊肘	gēbozhǒu	elbow; sleeve around elbow
6	补	bǔ	to mend, to patch
*7	补丁	bǔding	patch
*8	窜个儿	cuāngè(r)	to grow very quickly (kids)

9	瞎説	xiāshuō	胡説, blind or wild talk, nonsense
10	得了吧！	dé-le-ba!	no way! forget it
*11	粗布	cūbù	rough material, unrefined cloth
*12	混得	hùnde	doing, managing, to muddle along
*13	够嗆	gòuqiàng	很困難, tough enough; unbearable
14	困難	kùnnan	difficulty, hardship
*15	五七幹校	wǔqī gànxiào	May 7 Cadre Schools (schools established in the countryside in late 1968 where cadres were sent to do manual labor and study Mao's thought--so named because they were founded on the principles embodied in Mao's "May 7 Instructions")
16	勞動	láodòng	to labor

例句

A "嚷嚷" 是 "大叫" 的意思。例如：你小聲兒説好不好？別嚷嚷！

B 這種粗布料子做旗袍不合適。

C 嗐，這是甚麼料子啊？這麼粗，像蔴布袋似的。

D 我的胳膊肘很疼，今天不能打球。

E 這條褲子破了有一個洞，不能穿了。

　　我給補個補丁就能穿了。

　　我才不穿有補丁的褲子呢。

F 孩子長得很快叫 "竄個兒"。比方説：保羅正竄個兒呢，剛買的褲子就又短了，不能穿了。

G "瞎説" 是 "胡説，説的話沒有根據。" 例如：你瞎説。你怎麼知道美國每個人都有性病？

H 中國人在外國生活很困難啊！又得唸書又得作事，够嗆。

　　可是很多中國人都混得不錯啊，又買房子又買汽車。

89

9	瞎说	xiāshuō	胡说, blind or wild talk, nonsense
10	得了吧！	dé-le-ba!	no way! forget it
*11	粗布	cūbù	rough material, unrefined cloth
*12	混得	hùnde	doing, managing, to muddle along
*13	够呛	gòuqiàng	很困难, tough enough; unbearable
14	困难	kùnnan	difficulty, hardship
*15	五七干校	wǔqī gànxiào	May 7 Cadre Schools (schools established in the countryside in late 1968 where cadres were sent to do manual labor and study Mao's thought--so named because they were founded on the principles embodied in Mao's "May 7 Instructions")
16	劳动	láodòng	to labor

例句

A “嚷嚷”是“大叫”的意思。例如：你小声儿说好不好？别嚷嚷！

B 这种粗布料子做旗袍不合适。

C 嗨，这是甚么料子啊？这么粗，像麻布袋似的。

D 我的胳膊肘很疼，今天不能打球。

E 这条裤子破了有一个洞，不能穿了。
我给补个补丁就能穿了。
我才不穿有补丁的裤子呢。

F 孩子长得很快叫“蹿个儿”。比方说：保罗正蹿个儿呢，刚买的裤子就又短了，不能穿了。

G “瞎说”是“胡说，说的话没有根据。”例如：你瞎说。你怎么知道美国每个人都有性病？

H 中国人在外国生活很困难啊！又得念书又得作事，够呛。
可是很多中国人都混得不错啊，又买房子又买汽车。

得了吧！車，房子都是靠借債買的。

那算甚麼，在美國借錢是很流行的事。

I 文化大革命的時候，很多知識分子 zhīshi fènzi (intelligentsia)
到五七幹校去做甚麼？

勞動啊！

爲甚麼要勞動？

因爲毛主席説知識分子得向勞動人民學習啊！

得了吧！车，房子都是靠借债买的。

那算甚么，在美国借钱是很流行的事。

I 文化大革命的时候，很多知识分子 zhīshi fènzi (intelligentsia)
到五七干校去做甚么？

劳动啊！

为甚么要劳动？

因为毛主席说知识分子得向劳动人民学习啊！

練習八

一　課堂討論

1　爲甚麼現在莉莉不要她母親拆她的信了？莉莉告訴她母親不要再拆
　　看她的信的時候爲甚麼母親那麼生氣？

2　北京早晨的公園是一個很有意思的地方，請你形容一下那兒的情形。

3　保羅上不了公共汽車那一幕是要說明甚麼？

4　趙先生看見保羅敲他爸爸的頭的時候，很看不慣，爲甚麼？

5　太太在一塊兒的時候，談丈夫的事，先生在一塊兒的時候談太太甚麼事？

6　"京韻大鼓" Jīngyùn dàgǔ 是中國北京，天津一帶的一種民間音樂。
　　可惜現在很多人，尤其是年輕人都不喜歡也不懂這種音樂了。這一段是
　　駱玉笙 Luò Yù shēng 唱的。駱玉笙是現代中國四大京韻大鼓名家之一。
　　她唱的這一段大鼓名字叫擊鼓罵曹 jī-gǔ-mà-cáo (beat the drum and
　　rebuke) 曹操 Cáo Cao --- 三國演義 Sān Guó Yǎn Yì (The Romance o
　　the Three Kingdoms by Luò Guan-zhong)裏一段很有名的故事。
　　你想電影兒裏爲甚麼有這一幕呢？這一幕跟很多人在大雜院兒看電視有
　　甚麼關係嗎？

7　趙先生看了保羅穿的衣服以後就說方先生在美國的生活很困難，爲甚麼？

8　其他？

二　問答題

1　莉莉的媽媽爲甚麼覺得她應該拆她女兒的信？你父母拆看你的信嗎？

2　趙太太說她女兒"長翅膀了，盡拿洋文來矇我"是甚麼意思？

练习八

第四十一幕到第四十六幕

一　课堂讨论

1　为甚么现在莉莉不要她母亲拆她的信了？莉莉告诉她母亲不要再拆
　　看她的信的时候为甚么母亲那么生气？

2　北京早晨的公园是一个很有意思的地方，请你形容一下那儿的情形。

3　保罗上不了公共汽车那一幕是要说明甚么？

4　赵先生看见保罗敲他爸爸的头的时候，很看不惯，为甚么？

5　太太在一块儿的时候，谈丈夫的事，先生在一块儿的时候谈太太甚么事？

6　"京韵大鼓" Jīngyùn dàgǔ 是中国北京，天津一带的一种民间音乐。
　　可惜现在很多人，尤其是年轻人都不喜欢也不懂这种音乐了。这一段是
　　骆玉笙 Luò Yù shēng 唱的。骆玉笙是现代中国四大京韵大鼓名家之一。
　　她唱的这一段大鼓名字叫击鼓骂曹 Jī-gǔ-mà-cáo (beat the drum and
　　rebuke) 曹操 Cáo Cao --- 三国演义 Sān Guó Yǎn Yì (The Romance of
　　the Three Kingdoms by Luò Guan-zhong)裏一段很有名的故事。
　　你想电影儿裏为甚么有这一幕呢？这一幕跟很多人在大杂院儿看电视有
　　甚么关系吗？

7　赵先生看了保罗穿的衣服以后就说方先生在美国的生活很困难，为甚么？

8　其他？

二　问答题

1　莉莉的妈妈为甚么觉得她应该拆她女儿的信？你父母拆看你的信吗？

2　赵太太说她女儿"长翅膀了，尽拿洋文来蒙我"是甚么意思？

3   那天早上一達跟莉莉在公園說甚麼我們聽不見。你想他們說的是甚麼？

4   保羅爲甚麼上不上公共汽車？

5   趙先生說方先生的姐姐有甚麼毛病？

6   那天晚上我們怎麼知道趙先生跟方先生喝醉了？

7   你覺得中國的"京韻大鼓"怎麼樣？

8   爲甚麼趙先生想方先生沒錢給保羅買衣服？

9   保羅說他穿的衣服是甚麼樣的？

10   爲甚麼趙先生說他在五七幹校穿的褲子在美國會流行？

三   造句

1   往後：

2   瞞着：

3   翻譯：

4   當...面：

5   經驗：

6   料子：

3　那天早上一达跟莉莉在公园说甚么我们听不见。你想他们说的是甚么？

4　保罗为甚么上不上公共汽车？

5　赵先生说方先生的姐姐有甚么毛病？

6　那天晚上我们怎么知道赵先生跟方先生喝醉了？

7　你觉得中国的"京韵大鼓"怎么样？

8　为甚么赵先生想方先生没钱给保罗买衣服？

9　保罗说他穿的衣服是甚么样的？

10　为甚么赵先生说他在五七干校穿的裤子在美国会流行？

三　造句

1　往后：

2　瞒着：

3　翻译：

4　当...面：

5　经验：

6　料子：

7　瞎説：

8　得了吧！

9　困難：

10　勞動：

四　自由發揮

　　看了這個電影以後，你覺得<u>中美</u>兩國人，父母跟孩子之間的關係　有甚麼相同的地方？有甚麼不相同的地方？

7 瞎说：

8 得了吧！

9 困难：

10 劳动：

四 自由发挥

看了这个电影以后，你觉得<u>中美</u>两国人，父母跟孩子之间的关系 有甚么相同的地方？有甚么不相同的地方？

對白

第九節 Section Nine

第四十七幕到第五十幕 Scene 47 to Scene 50

In these three scenes a few more serious aspects of Chinese life are confronted. What has the Zhao family sacrificed, and why does Mrs. Zhao seem unconcerned? Consider whether Leo, Grace, and Paul are sensitive to the needs of their hosts. How does Lili like hanging out at the Beijing Hotel with the Americans?

第四十七幕 ---在趙家屋裏

趙太太：唉呀，你別老跟着我轉悠行不行啊？盡礙事。

趙先生：欸，我說，這莉莉就這麼玩兒，你管不管啊？

趙太太：你幹甚麼的？你幹嘛不管啊？

趙先生：這，我說得上話嗎？你們這母女倆心貼心的。自打你弟弟來了之後，就沒見她念過一天兒書。

趙太太：還早呢。

趙先生：還早呢？我翻了翻日曆，還有二十三天了。唉，整天就跟那個寶貝羅聽西洋歌曲，要不，就帶着耳機子蹦躂。我看着別扭。

趙太太：人家叫保羅，是個美國孩子，特活潑。

趙先生：哪國孩子也不成啊，沒上沒下的。那天我看他敲他爸爸的腦袋，你說有這樣的？欸，真的，抽空您跟您寶貝閨女提一提。

趙太太：怕甚麼呀，萬一考不取，讓小弟給她辦出國留學。

趙先生：你捨得就這麼一個寶貝閨女啊？

趙太太：唉，子女大了，就得各奔前程，再說，跟着自己親的舅舅，這有甚麼不放心的。

趙先生：唉，你，你懂甚麼，美國的社會啊，不知有多亂。治安不好，而且性關

94

对白

第九节 Section Nine

第四十七幕到第五十幕 Scene 47 to Scene 50

In these three scenes a few more serious aspects of Chinese life are confronted. What has the Zhao family sacrificed, and why does Mrs. Zhao seem unconcerned? Consider whether Leo, Grace, and Paul are sensitive to the needs of their hosts. How does Lili like hanging out at the Beijing Hotel with the Americans?

第四十七幕 ---在赵家屋裹

赵太太：唉呀，你别老跟着我转悠行不行啊？尽碍事。

赵先生：欸，我说，这莉莉就这么玩儿，你管不管啊？

赵太太：你干甚么的？你干嘛不管啊？

赵先生：这，我说得上话吗？你们这母女俩心贴心的。自打你弟弟来了之后，就没见她念过一天儿书。

赵太太：还早呢。

赵先生：还早呢？我翻了翻日历，还有二十三天了。唉，整天就跟那个宝贝罗听西洋歌曲，要不，就带着耳机子蹦跶。我看着别扭。

赵太太：人家叫保罗，是个美国孩子，特活泼。

赵先生：哪国孩子也不成啊，没上没下的。那天我看他敲他爸爸的脑袋，你说有这样的？欸，真的，抽空您跟您宝贝闺女提一提。

赵太太：怕甚么呀，万一考不取，让小弟给她办出国留学。

赵先生：你舍得就这么一个宝贝闺女啊？

赵太太：唉，子女大了，就得各奔前程，再说，跟着自己亲的舅舅，这有甚么不放心的。

赵先生：唉，你，你懂甚么，美国的社会啊，不知有多乱。治安不好，而且性关

94

係特亂，還有滿街的同性戀。弄不好啊，再帶回來個洋女婿。

第四十八幕 ---在北海業餘體校

第四十九幕 ---在北京飯店

洋人甲：How's your ping pong?

保羅：　My coach says I'm gonna be the best in the bunch, if I can just get my serve down. You know that singles title coming up? No problem, I'm gonna take it!

洋人乙：You're going to play against Liu? Lili, didn't your boyfriend Liu win the title last year?

洋人甲：Alright, this is going to be hot! Is it a major match?

保羅：　I don't know. It's major for me. Look at those two guys checking you out!

洋人乙：Look at this! They're really checking her out!

保羅：　What's a nice girl like you doing hanging around with foreign devils like us?

第五十幕 ---在趙家

保羅：　Mom, your favorite niece is in a funny mood. Again.

方太太：Stop teasing her! Give her some privacy.

保羅：　Oh, come on. I'm cool.

趙太太：我說啊，叫<u>莉莉</u>收拾桌子，馬上吃飯了。

趙先生：好。

方太太：Ready to move back to the hotel tonight?

保羅：　Not really. I'm kinda getting used to this place. Developing my leg muscles.

趙先生：<u>莉莉</u>，<u>莉莉</u>。

莉莉：　我不吃飯了。

系特乱，还有满街的同性恋。弄不好啊，再带回来个洋女婿。

第四十八幕 ---在北海业余体校

第四十九幕 ---在北京饭店

洋人甲： How's your ping pong?

保罗： My coach says I'm gonna be the best in the bunch, if I can just get my serve down. You know that singles title coming up? No problem, I'm gonna take it!

洋人乙： You're going to play against Liu? Lili, didn't your boyfriend Liu win the title last year?

洋人甲： Alright, this is going to be hot! Is it a major match?

保罗： I don't know. It's major for me. Look at those two guys checking you out!

洋人乙： Look at this! They're really checking her out!

保罗： What's a nice girl like you doing hanging around with foreign devils like us?

第五十幕 ---在赵家

保罗： Mom, your favorite niece is in a funny mood. Again.

方太太： Stop teasing her! Give her some privacy.

保罗： Oh, come on. I'm cool.

赵太太： 我说啊，叫莉莉收拾桌子，马上吃饭了。

赵先生： 好。

方太太： Ready to move back to the hotel tonight?

保罗： Not really. I'm kinda getting used to this place. Developing my leg muscles.

赵先生： 莉莉，莉莉。

莉莉： 我不吃饭了。

趙先生：我説啊，你管管你女兒吧。她説準備高考時間來不及了。

方太太：We're moving back to the hotel. Your father told me this
morning.

趙先生：從今兒起就不吃飯了。

保羅：　Why? Just because of Lily?

趙太太：胡説。

方太太：There is one thing in this country that causes more concern
than the Super Bowl game back home. The annual college
entrance examination.

保羅：　I know, I know. It's like a one in a hundred chance, and if
you don't make it then you have to sell tea in the streets.
Well, I think Lily'd make a beautiful tea pedlar.

方太太：Go inside and pack!!

赵先生：我说啊，你管管你女儿吧。她说准备高考时间来不及了。

方太太：We're moving back to the hotel. Your father told me this morning.

赵先生：从今儿起就不吃饭了。

保罗：　Why? Just because of Lily?

赵太太：胡说。

方太太：There is one thing in this country that causes more concern than the Super Bowl game back home. The annual college entrance examination.

保罗：　I know, I know. It's like a one in a hundred chance, and if you don't make it then you have to sell tea in the streets. Well, I think Lily'd make a beautiful tea pedlar.

方太太：Go inside and pack!!

生詞及例句

第四十七幕

生詞

1	哎呀	āiyā	(interjection showing dislike or disgust)
*2	轉悠	zhuànyou	to follow around
3	礙事	àishì	to get in one's way
4	管	guǎn	to concern oneself with another's business, to tell a child what to do
5	說得上話	shuō-de-shàng huà	not worth saying, won't do any good to say so
*6	心貼心	xīn-tiē-xīn	inseparable, very close to each other
7	自打... 以後	zìdǎ...yǐhòu	從... 以後, from here on
8	翻了翻	fān-le-fān	to flip through, to look through
9	日曆	rìlì	day calendar
10	寶貝	bǎobèi	treasure, precious one
11	要不	yàobù	要不然, otherwise
12	耳機子	ěrjīzi	walkman, earphones
*13	蹦躂	bèngda	跳, to jump around, to hop
14	看不慣	kàn-bu-guàn	can't get used to seeing, can't stand to see
15	人家	rénjia	other people, somebody else, they, he/she, I (This word, with the exclusion of the 2nd person "you,"

生词及例句

第四十七幕

生词

1	哎呀	āiyā	(interjection showing dislike or disgust)
*2	转悠	zhuànyou	to follow around
3	碍事	àishì	to get in one's way
4	管	guǎn	to concern oneself with another's business, to tell a child what to do
5	说得上话	shuō-de-shàng huà	not worth saying, won't do any good to say so
*6	心贴心	xīn-tiē-xīn	inseparable, very close to each other
7	自打...以后	zìdǎ...yǐhòu	从...以后, from here on
8	翻了翻	fān-le-fān	to flip through, to look through
9	日历	rìlì	day calendar
10	宝贝	bǎobèi	treasure, precious one
11	要不	yàobù	要不然, otherwise
12	耳机子	ěrjīzi	walkman, earphones
*13	蹦跶	bèngda	跳, to jump around, to hop
14	看不惯	kàn-bu-guàn	can't get used to seeing, can't stand to see
15	人家	rénjia	other people, somebody else, they, he/she, I (This word, with the exclusion of the 2nd person "you,"

represents person(s), specific
or generalized, singular or plural;
the exact meaning in the sentence
must be judged by its context.)

16	活潑	huópo	lively, active
*17	沒上沒下的	méishang-méi-xiàde	disrespectful and impolite behavior toward elders
*18	敲	qiāo	to knock
*19	腦袋	nǎodai	頭, head
20	抽空	chōukòng	to make time, to find time
21	提一提	tí-yi-tí	to mention, to bring up
22	萬一	wànyī	on the slight chance that (one in ten-thousand)
23	考不取	kǎo-bu-qǔ	考不上, to fail (entrance) exam and be rejected (by a school)
24	留學	liúxué	to study abroad
25	捨得	shěde	to let go
26	各奔前程	gè-bèn-qián-chéng	everyone goes their own way, each pursues her own goals (without caring about others)
27	治安	zhìān	public security, safety
28	性關係	xìng guānxi	sexual relations
29	同性戀	tóng xìng liàn	homosexuals
30	弄不好	nòng-bu-hǎo	to screw up, to ruin
31	洋女婿	yáng nǚxu	foreign son-in-law

例句

A "轉悠"是北京俗話，是"轉來轉去"的意思。

B 唉呀，這狗老躺在門口真礙事。你管管他好不好？
   我管不了．他不聽我的話。

16	活泼	huópo	lively, active
*17	没上没下的	méishàng-méixiàde	disrespectful and impolite behavior toward elders
*18	敲	qiāo	to knock
*19	脑袋	nǎodai	头，head
20	抽空	chōukòng	to make time, to find time
21	提一提	tí-yi-tí	to mention, to bring up
22	万一	wànyī	on the slight chance that (one in ten-thousand)
23	考不取	kǎo-bu-qǔ	考不上, to fail (entrance) exam and be rejected (by a school)
24	留学	liúxué	to study abroad
25	舍得	shěde	to let go
26	各奔前程	gè-bèn-qián-chéng	everyone goes their own way, each pursues her own goals (without caring about others)
27	治安	zhìān	public security, safety
28	性关系	xìng guānxi	sexual relations
29	同性恋	tóng xìng liàn	homosexuals
30	弄不好	nòng-bu-hǎo	to screw up, to ruin
31	洋女婿	yáng nǚxu	foreign son-in-law

例句

A "转悠"是北京俗话，是"转来转去"的意思。

B 唉呀，这狗老躺在门口真碍事。你管管他好不好？
　我管不了。他不听我的话。

C “説得上話嘛”意思是“説了話也沒用，説了他也不聽。”

D “心貼心”是説“兩個人的關係很近，好像他們心是貼在一起的。”

E “自打”是“自從”的意思。所以“自打你走了以後”，就是“自從你走了以後”的意思。

F 請你翻翻日曆，看看你舅舅的生日是星期幾？

G 別把孩子當寶貝，弄不好啊，你會把孩子慣壞了。

H 我們去看電影兒好嗎？要不，去跳舞也行。

I 年輕人喜歡戴着耳機子一邊聽音樂，一邊蹦躂。

J 趙先生看保羅敲他爸爸的腦袋，覺得美國孩子沒上沒下的，太沒禮貌，他看不（習）慣，因為在中國孩子不可以隨便打父親的頭。

K 請你跟趙太太提一提，抽空給我做一件衣服好嗎？

人家才沒工夫給你做衣服呢。

L 我連大學都考不取，怎麼能出國留學？

M 我已經跟他提過了。他説他捨不得你走。怕你萬一走了不回來了怎麼辦？

N 我們小時候是好朋友，可是考取大學以後，就各奔前程，沒再見面了。

O 在大城市裏治安不好，你最好晚上不要一個人出去。

P 現在男女性關係很隨便，再説同性戀的人也很多，所以得愛滋病的人越來越多。

Q “洋”是“外國”的意思，“女婿”是“女兒的丈夫”，所以“洋女婿”就是女兒的丈夫是外國人。

第五十幕

生詞

1	收拾桌子	shōushi zhuōzi	to set the table; to clear the table
2	胡説	húshuō	to talk nonsense or rubbish

例句

C "说得上话嘛"意思是"说了话也没用，说了他也不听。"

D "心贴心"是说"两个人的关系很近，好像他们心是贴在一起的。"

E "自打"是"自从"的意思。所以"自打你走了以后"，就是"自从你走了以后"的意思。

F 请你翻翻日历，看看你舅舅的生日是星期几？

G 别把孩子当宝贝，弄不好啊，你会把孩子惯坏了。

H 我们去看电影儿好吗？要不，去跳舞也行。

I 年轻人喜欢戴着耳机子一边听音乐，一边蹦跶。

J 赵先生看保罗敲他爸爸的脑袋，觉得美国孩子没上没下的，太没礼貌，他看不（习）惯，因为在中国孩子不可以随便打父亲的头。

K 请你跟赵太太提一提，抽空给我做一件衣服好吗？
   人家才没工夫给你做衣服呢。

L 我连大学都考不取，怎么能出国留学？

M 我已经跟他提过了。他说他舍不得你走。怕你万一走了不回来了怎么办？

N 我们小时候是好朋友，可是考取大学以后，就各奔前程，没再见面了。

O 在大城市裹治安不好，你最好晚上不要一个人出去。

P 现在男女性关系很随便，再说同性恋的人也很多，所以得爱滋病的人越来越多。

Q "洋"是"外国"的意思，"女婿"是"女儿的丈夫"，所以"洋女婿"就是女儿的丈夫是外国人。

第五十幕

生词

| 1 | 收拾桌子 | shōushi zhuōzi | to set the table; to clear the table |
| 2 | 胡说 | húshuō | to talk nonsense or rubbish |

例句

A 快吃飯了，趙太太叫莉莉收拾桌子，擺上碗筷。

B 不知道的事情不可以胡説。

C 我考不上大學就要自殺。

D 胡説！

A 快吃饭了，<u>赵</u>太太叫<u>莉莉</u>收拾桌子，摆上碗筷。

B 不知道的事情不可以<u>胡说</u>。

C 我考不上大学就要自杀。

D <u>胡说</u>！

練習九

一　課堂討論

1　從第四十七幕趙先生跟趙太太的談話，請你說一說一般中國人
　(1)　對美國的看法。
　(2)　對在美國長大的中國孩子的看法。
　(3)　對有"海外關係"的看法。
2　一般中國人對中國女孩子跟美國男孩子交朋友的看法。
3　爲甚麼方家決定要搬到旅館去住？保羅爲甚麼現在不願意搬走了？
4　保羅能不能了解在中國考上大學的重要？你呢？
5　請你形容一下高考的前幾天莉莉的情形。
6　其他？

二　問答題

1　爲甚麼趙先生要跟着趙太太直轉？

2　爲甚麼莉莉現在不用功了？

3　趙先生喜歡保羅嗎？你怎麼知道？

4　對莉莉考大學的事，爲甚麼趙太太沒有趙先生那麼着急？

5　趙太太爲甚麼決定不讓莉莉到美國去了？

6　方太太告訴保羅甚麼？保羅在趙家習慣了嗎？

练习九

一　课堂讨论

1　从第四十七幕赵先生跟赵太太的谈话，请你说一说一般中国人

（1）　对美国的看法。

（2）　对在美国长大的中国孩子的看法。

（3）　对有"海外关系"的看法。

2　一般中国人对中国女孩子跟美国男孩子交朋友的看法。

3　为甚么方家决定要搬到旅馆去住？保罗为甚么现在不愿意搬走了？

4　保罗能不能了解在中国考上大学的重要？你呢？

5　请你形容一下高考的前几天莉莉的情形。

6　其他？

二　问答题

1　为甚么赵先生要跟着赵太太直转？

2　为甚么莉莉现在不用功了？

3　赵先生喜欢保罗吗？你怎么知道？

4　对莉莉考大学的事，为甚么赵太太没有赵先生那么着急？

5　赵太太为甚么决定不让莉莉到美国去了？

6　方太太告诉保罗甚么？保罗在赵家习惯了吗？

7 方太太説<u>中國</u>的高考跟<u>美國</u>的甚麼一樣重要？

8 <u>趙太太</u>叫<u>莉莉</u>做甚麼？

9 <u>莉莉</u>爲甚麼不吃飯了？

10 你想爲甚麼<u>趙先生</u>自己不管<u>莉莉</u>？在你們家是你爸爸管孩子還是你媽媽管孩子？

三 造句

1 自打...以後：

2 要不（然）：

3 看不慣：

4 活潑：

5 抽空：

6 提一提：

7 萬一：

8 捨得：

9 治安：

10 待（一）會兒：

7 　 方太太说<u>中国</u>的高考跟<u>美国</u>的甚么一样重要？

8 　 <u>赵</u>太太叫<u>莉莉</u>做甚么？

9 　 <u>莉莉</u>为甚么不吃饭了？

10 　 你想为甚么<u>赵</u>先生自己不管<u>莉莉</u>？在你们家是你爸爸管孩子
　　 还是你妈妈管孩子？

三　造句

1 　 自打... 以后：

2 　 要不（然）：

3 　 看不惯：

4 　 活泼：

5 　 抽空：

6 　 提一提：

7 　 万一：

8 　 舍得：

9 　 治安：

10 　 待（一）会儿：

四 翻譯

1 We're moving back to the hotel. Your father told me this
  morning.

2 Why? Just because of Lily? I'm kinda getting used to this
  place.

3 The annual college entrance examination in this country
  causes more concern than the Super Bowl game back home.

4 I know, I know. It's like a one-in-a-hundred chance, and if
  you don't make it then you have to sell tea in the streets.

5 Go inside and pack!

五 自由發揮

你想莉莉會到美國去嗎？為甚麼？

四　翻译

1　We're moving back to the hotel. Your father told me this
　morning.

2　Why? Just because of Lily? I'm kinda getting used to this
　place.

3　The annual college entrance examination in this country
　causes more concern than the Super Bowl game back home.

4　I know, I know. It's like a one-in-a-hundred chance, and if
　you don't make it then you have to sell tea in the streets.

5　Go inside and pack!

五　自由发挥

　　你想莉莉会到美国去吗？为甚么？

對白

第十節 Section Ten

第五十一幕到第六十一幕 Scene 51 to Scene 61

Yida and Lili seem suddenly motivated to diligent study. Lili, however, handles the pressure differently. How does her family try to help her? In what ways were the families affected by their time together? Keeping in mind the intentions of the writers, is this a tragic or victorious ending?

第五十一幕 ---在莉莉臥房

趙太太： 莉莉，莉莉，出來吃飯！

莉莉： 唉呀，媽，我跟你說過了，高考之前我不出房門。

趙太太： 呀！這屋怎麼搞成這樣？像農貿市場似的。來！快把這碗豬肝湯喝了！

莉莉： 我不喝。

趙太太： 快接過來！快！燙着你媽手了。快點兒！哎喲！

莉莉： 你說，我高考之前背生字，還來得及嗎？

趙太太： 欸，先把這碗豬肝湯喝完了。這不吃飯哪行啊！"人是鐵，飯是鋼"，一頓不吃都不行。欸，趁熱喝了！

第五十二幕 ---高考前夕在劉家

劉先生： 甚麼時候了，睡吧！

一達： 再待一會兒。

第五十三幕 ---高考前夕在趙家

趙太太： 豬肝湯喝了不上兩口。

104

对白

第十节 Section Ten

第五十一幕到第六十一幕 Scene 51 to Scene 61

Yida and Lili seem suddenly motivated to diligent study. Lili, however, handles the pressure differently. How does her family try to help her? In what ways were the families affected by their time together? Keeping in mind the intentions of the writers, is this a tragic or victorious ending?

第五十一幕 ---在莉莉卧房

赵太太：莉莉，莉莉，出来吃饭！

莉莉：　 唉呀，妈，我跟你说过了，高考之前我不出房门。

赵太太：呀！这屋怎么搞成这样？像农贸市场似的。来！快把这碗猪肝汤喝了！

莉莉：　 我不喝。

赵太太：快接过来！快！烫着你妈手了。快点儿！哎哟！

莉莉：　 你说，我高考之前背生字，还来得及吗？

赵太太：欸，先把这碗猪肝汤喝完了。这不吃饭哪行啊！"人是铁，饭是钢"，一顿不吃都不行。欸，趁热喝了！

第五十二幕 ---高考前夕在刘家

刘先生：甚么时候了，睡吧！

一达：　 再待一会儿。

第五十三幕 ---高考前夕在赵家

赵太太：猪肝汤喝了不上两口。

趙先生：　你那豬肝湯啊，真不怎麼好喝。

趙太太：　這幾天她真的連房門都不出，廁所都沒上，怎麼得了啊！

趙先生：　不吃不喝，也就不拉不撒。

第五十四幕 ---在莉莉臥房

莉莉：　　... 媽媽！媽媽！

趙先生：　我說，....

第五十五幕 ---在考場

第五十六幕 ---在劉家

載華：　　兩點鐘了，起不起？沒氣兒了，沒氣兒。

一達：　　手往哪兒擱過了，邪臭，邪臭的。

載華：　　沒味兒啊！出去逛逛。老待在家幹嘛啊？活動，活動。

一達：　　幹甚麼？高考也過了，要考還得等到明年呢。

載華：　　聽聽這個。

鄰居：　　別唱了。嚇得小三尿炕了。

載華：　　聽說莉莉出院了。哪天咱們看看她去。人家現在跟咱們一樣也是待業
　　　　　青年了。教練讓你練球去。

一達：　　大熱天，練甚麼球？

載華：　　就要比賽了。

一達：　　So what?

載華：　　教練說了，你要不好好練球兒，參加比賽，冠軍非叫方保羅那寶貝給
　　　　　端了。

第五十七幕 ---在北海業餘體校

教練：　　你這球打得不錯，挺有進步的。好好練習。

保羅：　　謝謝。

赵先生：你那猪肝汤啊，真不怎么好喝。

赵太太：这几天她真的连房门都不出，厕所都没上，怎么得了啊！

赵先生：不吃不喝，也就不拉不撒。

第五十四幕 ---在莉莉卧房

莉莉：　　...妈妈！妈妈！

赵先生：我说，....

第五十五幕 ---在考场

第五十六幕 ---在刘家

载华：　　两点钟了，起不起？没气儿了，没气儿。

一达：　　手往哪儿搁过了，邪臭，邪臭的。

载华：　　没味儿啊！出去逛逛。老待在家干嘛啊？活动，活动。

一达：　　干甚么？高考也过了，要考还得等到明年呢。

载华：　　听听这个。

邻居：　　别唱了。吓得<u>小三</u>尿炕了。

载华：　　听说<u>莉莉</u>出院了。哪天咱们看看她去。人家现在跟咱们一样也是待业
　　　　　青年了。教练让你练球去。

一达：　　大热天，练甚么球？

载华：　　就要比赛了。

一达：　　So what?

载华：　　教练说了，你要不好好练球儿，参加比赛，冠军非叫<u>方保罗</u>那宝贝给
　　　　　端了。

第五十七幕 ---在北海业余体校

教练：　　你这球打得不错，挺有进步的。好好练习。

保罗：　　谢谢。

第五十八幕 ---賽球

報告員：<u>方保羅</u>是<u>美國加州</u>少年組冠軍。另一位決賽員是<u>劉一達</u>。

第五十九幕 ---在體育館更衣室

方先生：How do you feel, dick breath?

保羅：　Oh, great. Just great.

方先生：You had a tough match tonight. Didn't you?

保羅：　I play to win. I hate losing. I hate it so much.

方先生：Listen, son, you see...you played the best game ever. Well, you didn't win the championship. You gave the best performance, the best shots, and that's a victory by itself. Can you understand that? You see, in each tournament there's only one champ, but many winners. I think today you are one of them, winners...

保羅：　Dad, I'm kinda hungry, you know. So, why don't you save your bullshit.

方先生：Okay, why don't you let me treat you to one of those grand Peking duck feast with a warm Coca-Cola?

保羅：　Okay. You know, if you wanna say it right, you gotta say penis breath...

第六十幕 ---在劉家門前慶祝一達考上大學

第六十一幕--- 在方家

Wilson: Hi Grace!

方太太：Mr. Wilson, what a surprise.

Wilson: My, you look lovely.

方太太：Thank you, it's a Chinese peasant blouse.

第五十八幕 ---赛球

报告员：方保罗是美国加州少年组冠军。另一位决赛员是刘一达。

第五十九幕 ---在体育馆更衣室

方先生： How do you feel, dick breath?

保罗：　Oh, great. Just great.

方先生： You had a tough match tonight. Didn't you?

保罗：　I play to win. I hate losing. I hate it so much.

方先生： Listen, son, you see...you played the best game ever. Well, you didn't win the championship. You gave the best performance, the best shots, and that's a victory by itself. Can you understand that? You see, in each tournament there's only one champ, but many winners. I think today you are one of them, winners...

保罗：　Dad, I'm kinda hungry, you know. So, why don't you save your bullshit.

方先生： Okay, why don't you let me treat you to one of those grand Peking duck feast with a warm Coca-Cola?

保罗：　Okay. You know, if you wanna say it right, you gotta say penis breath...

第六十幕 ---在刘家门前庆祝一达考上大学

第六十一幕--- 在方家

Wilson: Hi Grace!

方太太： Mr. Wilson, what a surprise.

Wilson: My, you look lovely.

方太太： Thank you, it's a Chinese peasant blouse.

Wilson: Elegant.

方太太: Do come in.

Wilson: How was your trip to China?

方太太: Oh, it was wonderful.

保羅: People in America think I'm too Chinese, and then people in China think I'm too American. What do you think about that? Bossman!

Linda: Meiyoo, meiyo.

保羅: No, you have to say "沒有"。我們這兒沒有。

方太太: The Chinese doctors stuck needles in his back. It gave him a funny tingling sensation, but it worked. Worked like a charm.

Wilson: Magic, magic. Looking good Liu!

劇終

Wilson: Elegant.

方太太: Do come in.

Wilson: How was your trip to China?

方太太: Oh, it was wonderful.

保罗: People in America think I'm too Chinese, and then people in
China think I'm too American. What do you think about that?
Bossman!

Linda: Meiyoo, meiyo.

保罗: No, you have to say "没有"。我们这儿没有。

方太太: The Chinese doctors stuck needles in his back. It gave him
a funny tingling sensation, but it worked. Worked like a
charm.

Wilson: Magic, magic. Looking good Liu!

剧终

生詞及例句

第五十一幕

生詞

*1	農貿市場	nóngmàoshìchǎng	free market for farmers (here used to describe a mess)
*2	豬肝湯	zhūgān tāng	pork liver soup
3	燙着	tàngzhe	to burn, to scald
4	哎喲	āiyo	(interjection of surprise at something unpleasant)
5	背	bèi	to memorize
6	來得及	lái-de-jí	to have enough time to
*7	人是鐵，飯是鋼	rén-shi-tiě, fàn-shi-gāng	one needs food for strength (people are iron, food is steel)
8	頓	dùn	(measure word for meals)
9	趁熱	chèn rè	while it's hot

例句

A　"農貿市場"是中國最近才有的的自由市場。每天農人把自己出產的東西拿到農貿市場去賣。那兒常常很髒很亂。趙太太看見莉莉的屋子亂七八糟，所以說"像農貿市場一樣."

B　中國人想，吃豬肝對人身體很好，最近莉莉唸書很辛苦，所以媽媽特意給莉莉做豬肝湯給她吃。

C　這是開水，很燙 (boiling hot)。小心！別燙着你的手。

D　哎喲！　燙着我的手了。疼死了。

E　明天考試現在背生字來得及嗎？
　　得看有多少生字，要是生字不多還來得及，要是多就來不及了。

生词及例句

生词

*1	农贸市场	nóngmàoshìchǎng	free market for farmers (here used to describe a mess)
*2	猪肝汤	zhūgān tāng	pork liver soup
3	烫着	tàngzhe	to burn, to scald
4	哎哟	āiyo	(interjection of surprise at something unpleasant)
5	背	bèi	to memorize
6	来得及	lái-de-jí	to have enough time to
*7	人是铁， 饭是钢	rén-shi-tiě, fàn-shi-gāng	one needs food for strength (people are iron, food is steel)
8	顿	dùn	(measure word for meals)
9	趁热	chèn rè	while it's hot

例句

A　"农贸市场"是中国最近才有的的自由市场。每天农人把自己出产的东西拿到农贸市场去卖。那儿常常很脏很乱。赵太太看见莉莉的屋子乱七八糟，所以说"像农贸市场一样."

B　中国人想，吃猪肝对人身体很好，最近莉莉念书很辛苦，所以妈妈特意给莉莉做猪肝汤给她吃。

C　这是开水，很烫 (boiling hot)。小心！别烫着你的手。

D　哎哟！　烫着我的手了。疼死了。

E　明天考试现在背生字来得及吗？
　　得看有多少生字，要是生字不多还来得及，要是多就来不及了。

F "人是鐵，飯是鋼"的意思是如果人要身體好，一定得吃東西。飯是很要緊的。

G 豬肝湯一定得趁熱喝，要不然就不好喝了。

第五十二幕

生詞

1 前夕   qián xī   the night before, the eve of
2 待一會兒   dāi yìhuǐ(r)   等一會兒, wait a minute

例句

A "前夕"是"某天的前一個晚上。"比方說六月四號是高考，高考的前夕就是六月三號的晚上。

B "待一會兒"在這兒是"等一會兒"的意思。

第五十三幕

生詞

1   不上   bú shàng   not quite
2   兩口   liǎng kǒu   two mouthfuls
3   廁所   cèsuǒ   toilet, bathroom
4   沒上   méi shàng   didn't go, hasn't gone
*5 不拉不撒 bù-lā-bù-sā   neither poop nor pee

例句

A "不上"是北京話"不到"的意思。比方說："不上兩天"，就是"不到兩天"的意思。

109

F　"人是铁，饭是钢"的意思是如果人要身体好，一定得吃东西。饭是很要紧的。

G　猪肝汤一定得趁热喝，要不然就不好喝了。

第五十二幕

生词

1	前夕	qián xī	the night before, the eve of
2	待一会儿	dāi yihuǐ(r)	等一会儿，wait a minute

例句

A　"前夕"是"某天的前一个晚上。"比方说六月四号是高考，高考的前夕就是六月三号的晚上。

B　"待一会儿"在这儿是"等一会儿"的意思。

第五十三幕

生词

1	不上	bú shàng	not quite
2	两口	liǎng kǒu	two mouthfuls
3	厕所	cèsuǒ	toilet, bathroom
4	没上	méi shàng	didn't go, hasn't gone
*5	不拉不撒	bù-lā-bù-sā	neither poop nor pee

例句

A　"不上"是北京话"不到"的意思。比方说："不上两天"，就是"不到两天"的意思。

B　那個菜不好吃，他吃了兩口就不吃了。

C　請問，廁所在哪兒？

　　男廁所還是女廁所？

　　我是女的。你說我要上男廁所還是女廁所？

D　"不拉不撒"的意思是"也不大便也不小便。"因爲莉莉沒吃東西也沒

　　喝水，當然她就不拉不撒了。

第五十六幕

生詞

1	活動	huódòng	to be active; activities
2	參加	cānjīa	to participate, to join in
3	比賽	bǐsài	to compete; competition, game
4	冠軍	guànjūn	the title of champion, winner
5	非叫	fēi jiào	一定叫, to insist that
*6	給端了	gěi-duān-le	給拿去了, to be taken by

例句

A　那個學生很活動，他甚麼活動都喜歡參加。

B　學校有甚麼課外活動 kèwài huódòng (extracurricular)　我們

　　可以參加嗎？

　　有乒乓球比賽，也有足球比賽。教練說，這次你一定得參加。

　　爲甚麼非叫我參加呢？

　　因爲只有你有希望得到冠軍，所以你非參加不可。你不願意冠軍讓

　　別人給端去吧？

第五十八幕

生詞

B　那个菜不好吃，他吃了两口就不吃了。

C　请问，厕所在哪儿？

男厕所还是女厕所？

我是女的。你说我要上男厕所还是女厕所？

D　"不拉不撒"的意思是"也不大便也不小便。"因为莉莉没吃东西也没喝水，当然她就不拉不撒了。

第五十六幕

生词

1	活动	huódòng	to be active; activities
2	参加	cānjiā	to participate, to join in
3	比赛	bǐsài	to compete; competition, game
4	冠军	guànjūn	the title of champion, winner
5	非叫	fēi jiào	一定叫，to insist that
*6	给端了	gěi-duān-le	给拿去了，to be taken by

例句

A　那个学生很活动，他甚么活动都喜欢参加。

B　学校有甚么课外活动 kèwài huódòng (extracurricular)　我们可以参加吗？

有乒乓球比赛，也有足球比赛。教练说，这次你一定得参加。

为甚么非叫我参加呢？

因为只有你有希望得到冠军，所以你非参加不可。你不愿意冠军让别人给端去吧？

第五十八幕

生词

| 1 | 賽球 | sài qiú | ballgame |
| *2 | 決賽員 | juésài yuán | finalist |

例句

A 那天賽球有幾個決賽員？
就兩個。一個是美國的方保羅，一個是中國的劉一達。
誰打得好？
都打得很好。冠軍最後是讓誰給端去了？
一達。

第五十九幕

生詞

| 1 | 更衣室 | gēng-yī shì | locker room, dressing room |

例句

"更衣室"是"換衣服的屋子"。比方説：球員都在更衣室換衣服。

第六十幕

生詞

| 1 | 慶祝 | qìngzhù | to celebrate |

例句

A 那天爲甚麼有很多人在一達家門口？

111

1	赛球	sài qiú	ballgame
*2	决赛员	juésài yuán	finalist

例句

A 那天赛球有几个决赛员？
就两个。一个是美国的方保罗，一个是中国的刘一达。
谁打得好？
都打得很好。冠军最后是让谁给端去了？
一达。

第五十九幕

生词

1	更衣室	gēng-yī shì	locker room, dressing room

例句

"更衣室"是"换衣服的屋子"。比方说：球员都在更衣室换衣服。

第六十幕

生词

1	庆祝	qìngzhù	to celebrate

例句

A 那天为甚么有很多人在一达家门口？

111

因爲在中國能考上大學是很不容易的事，也是很光榮 guāngróng
(glory) 的事，所以鄰居知道劉一達考上了大學，都來給他慶祝。

莉莉考上了沒有？

沒有。她病了，沒能參加考試。你看見了沒有？那天她也來看一達了。

看見了，看見了。

欸，你想他們倆以後會怎麼樣？

那還不是明擺着的嗎？

因为在中国能考上大学是很不容易的事，也是很光荣 guāngróng
（glory）的事，所以邻居知道刘一达考上了大学，都来给他庆祝。

莉莉考上了没有？

没有。她病了，没能参加考试。你看见了没有？那天她也来看一达了。

看见了，看见了。

欸，你想他们俩以后会怎么样？

那还不是明摆着的吗？

練習十

一 課堂討論

1 莉莉有沒有參加高考？為甚麼？

2 為甚麼一達決定要參加乒乓球比賽？

3 請你說一說那場球賽的情形。

4 方先生是不是一個好爸爸？為甚麼？

5 為甚麼很多人在劉家的門前？

6 電影兒最後是怎麼結局的？要是你是這個電影兒的導演你要怎麼結局？

7 這次方家到中國去旅行，對趙家方家的人有甚麼影響？

二 問答題

1 趙太太說莉莉這兩天怎麼樣？

2 莉莉為甚麼沒參加高考？

3 一達考完了以後，他爸爸給他一瓶甚麼？

4 高考以後，一達成天做甚麼？

5 甚麼人參加了乒乓球決賽？

6 這場乒乓球賽誰輸了？他爸爸跟他說甚麼？

7 你想莉莉跟一達還是好朋友嗎？你怎麼知道？

练习十

第五十一幕到第六十一幕

一　课堂讨论

1　莉莉有没有参加高考？为甚么？

2　为甚么一达决定要参加乒乓球比赛？

3　请你说一说那场球赛的情形。

4　方先生是不是一个好爸爸？为甚么？

5　为甚么很多人在刘家的门前？

6　电影儿最后是怎么结局的？要是你是这个电影儿的导演你要怎么结局？

7　这次方家到中国去旅行，对赵家方家的人有甚么影响？

二　问答题

1　赵太太说莉莉这两天怎么样？

2　莉莉为甚么没参加高考？

3　一达考完了以后，他爸爸给他一瓶甚么？

4　高考以后，一达成天做甚么？

5　甚么人参加了乒乓球决赛？

6　这场乒乓球赛谁输了？他爸爸跟他说甚么？

7　你想莉莉跟一达还是好朋友吗？你怎么知道？

8　　保罗从中国回来以后，有甚么感想？

9　　方先生现在太极拳打得怎么样？你怎么知道？

10　你想为甚么 Mr. Wilson 去找方先生？

三 造句

1　厕所：

2　上：

3　活动：

4　参加：

5　比赛：

6　非叫：

7　给 (verb) 了：

8　冠军：

9　更衣室：

10　庆祝：

四　自由发挥

请你形容一下中国学生参加高考前后的情形

8　　保羅從中國回來以後，有甚麼感想？

9　　方先生現在太極拳打得怎麼樣？你怎麼知道？

10　你想為甚麼 Mr. Wilson 去找方先生？

三 造句

1　　廁所：

2　　上：

3　　活動：

4　　參加：

5　　比賽：

6　　非叫：

7　　給 (verb) 了：

8　　冠軍：

9　　更衣室：

10　慶祝：

四　自由發揮

請你形容一下中國學生參加高考前後的情形

總複習

1 請你把這個故事的大意寫出來。

2 請你批評批評這個電影。

3 你喜歡這個電影的結局 jiéjú (ending) 嗎？
如果你是編劇人你要怎麼結局？

4 這次<u>方</u>家到<u>北京</u>去探親 tànqīn (visit relatives)，
對他們兩家有甚麼影響？

总复习

1 请你把这个故事的大意写出来。

2 请你批评批评这个电影。

3 你喜欢这个电影的结局 jiéjú (ending) 吗？
如果你是编剧人你要怎么结局？

4 这次方家到北京去探亲 tànqīn (visit relatives)，
对他们两家有甚么影响？

拼音索引

Phonetic Index

Entries are indexed by *scene* and *vocabulary number*. Asterisks indicate optional vocabulary.

A

āhā	啊哈	27.05
ài↘	唉	05.01
ai↘	欸	01.05
ǎi	矮	04.11
àishì	碍事	47.03
āiyā	哎呀	47.01
āiyō	哎哟	51.04
àndì	暗地	19.03
ānpái	安排	05.08

B

bàn jīn	半斤	44.17
bāng	帮	23.09
bǎobèi	宝贝	47.10
bā-chéng	八成	05.18
bèi	背	51.05
bèngda	* 蹦躂	47.13
biǎogē	表哥	32.03
bǐjì běn	笔记本	12.06
bìngbu zěnme	并不怎么	27.03
bīnglěng	冰冷	09.20
bīngliáng	冰凉	09.21
bǐsài	比赛	56.03
bù juéde	不觉得	36.05

116

bú shàng	不上	53.01
bǔ	補	46.06
bǔdīng	＊補丁	46.07
bùguǎn...dōu	不管...都	33.04
bújiùshìle	不就是了	05.12
búshì...jiùshì	不是...就是	13.05
bǔxí bān	＊補習班	04.03
bùxīng	不興	36.06
bù-lā-bù-sā	＊不拉不撒	53.05

C

cái...bù ne	才...不呢	25.11
cán dòu	＊蠶豆	28.18
cānjiā	參加	56.02
cèsuǒ	廁所	53.03
chā	插	25.09
chà	差	40.13
chá	查	05.20
chà diǎn(r)	差點兒	15.17
chāi	拆	41.02
chāichú	拆除	22.08
chángchang	嚐嚐	09.03
chèn rè	趁熱	51.09
chéng qiáng	城牆	22.01
chěng néng	逞能	36.07
chéngtiān	成天	36.01
chī-bu-liǎo	吃不了	24.09
cnóngxīn	重新	05.11
chōukòng	抽空	47.20
chū qī	初期	22.03

bú shàng	不上	53.01
bǔ	补	46.06
bǔdīng	*补丁	46.07
bùguǎn...dōu	不管...都	33.04
bújiùshìle	不就是了	05.12
búshi...jiùshi	不是...就是	13.05
bǔxí bān	*补习班	04.03
bùxīng	不兴	36.06
bù-lā-bù-sǎ	*不拉不撒	53.05

C

cái...bù ne	才...不呢	25.11
cán dòu	*蚕豆	28.18
cānjiā	参加	56.02
cèsuǒ	厕所	53.03
chā	插	25.09
chà	差	40.13
chá	查	05.20
chà diǎn(r)	差点儿	15.17
chāi	拆	41.02
chāichú	拆除	22.08
chángchang	尝尝	09.03
chèn rè	趁热	51.09
chéng qiáng	城墙	22.01
chěng néng	逞能	36.07
chéngtiān	成天	36.01
chī-bù-liǎo	吃不了	24.09
chóngxīn	重新	05.11
chōukòng	抽空	47.20
chū qī	初期	22.03

117

dé-le-ba!	得了吧	46.10
diàn tǎn	電毯	25.06
diànmén	電門	25.10
diàn yā	電壓	27.12
diē	爹	36.13
dìmèi	弟妹	37.07
dǐng	頂	19.04
diūrén	丟人	19.01
dòng	洞	35.04
dúbái	獨白	19.08
dūcù	督促	40.05
duìfu	對付	04.06
dùn	頓	51.08
duō	多	09.15
dùzi	肚子	38.07
dú-sǐ-shū	讀死書	40.17

E

ěrjīzi	耳機子	47.12

F

fàn guī	犯規	33.03
fānyì	翻譯	41.04
fǎnzhèng	反正	13.07
fān-le-fān	翻了翻	47.08
fēijiào	非叫	56.05
Fēilùbīn	菲律賓	23.10
fúqì	福氣	09.16
fùxí	複習	40.06

dé-le-ba!	得了吧	46.10
diàn tǎn	电毯	25.06
diànmén	电门	25.10
diàn yā	电压	27.12
diē	爹	36.13
dìmèi	弟妹	37.07
dǐng	顶	19.04
diūrén	丢人	19.01
dòng	洞	35.04
dúbái	独白	19.08
dūcù	督促	40.05
duìfu	对付	04.06
dùn	顿	51.08
duō	多	09.15
dùzi	肚子	38.07
dú-sǐ-shū	读死书	40.17

E

ěrjīzi	耳机子	47.12

F

fàn guī	犯规	33.03
fānyì	翻译	41.04
fǎnzhèng	反正	13.07
fān-le-fān	翻了翻	47.08
fēijiào	非叫	56.05
Fēilùbīn	菲律宾	23.10
fúqì	福气	09.16
fùxí	复习	40.06

gǎnjué	感覺	19.10
gànma?	幹嘛?	04.01
gǎnshang	趕上	24.03
gǎnxiǎng	感想	19.15
gǎo cuòle	搞錯了	27.11
gāo kǎo	高考	05.10
gāo gàn	高幹	23.13
gē	擱	09.12
gēbozhǒu	胳膊肘	46.05
gěi-duān-le	*給端了	56.06
gējù	歌劇	13.15
gēn...nàofān	跟...鬧翻	36.18
gēn...shìde	跟...似的	28.16
gēng-nián-qī	更年期	44.08
gēng-yī shì	更衣室	59.01
gērmen	*哥兒們	09.07
gè-bēn-qián-chéng	各奔前程	47.26
gōngsī	公司	36.16
gòu	搆	0C.18
gōuda	勾搭	04.08
gòuqiàng	*够嗆	46.13
guǎn	管	47.04
guàng	逛	19.14
guāng	*光	05.19
guànjūn	冠軍	56.04
gǔdao	*鼓搗	25.05
gūfù	姑父	23.08
guīnü	*閨女	15.03

guō	鍋	24.08
guòqù	過去	29.01
guówù yuàn	國務院	22.06
gǔ-jīn-zhōng-wài	古今中外	44.07

H

hāhā	哈哈	02.06
hài↘	嗐	46.03
hái bùrú	還不如	34.01
hái...ne	還...呢	25.03
hǎiwài guānxi	海外關係	23.11
hái-bù-jiù-nàma-yàng?	還不就那麼樣？	40.02
hǎn	喊	23.06
hei↗	嘿	09.09
heng/hng↘	哼	41.08
heng/hng↗	哼	13.06
héshì	合適	37.04
hēzuìle	喝醉了	44.13
hōu	*齁	24.11
huài máobìng	壞毛病	36.12
huàn	換	35.01
huānyíng	歡迎	23.04
huítóu	回頭	12.04
hūlu	*呼嚕	27.01
húnào	胡鬧	27.07
hùnde	混得	46.12
huò	貨	27.08
huǒ zàng	火葬	28.14
huódòng	活動	56.01

121

guō	锅	24.08
guòqù	过去	29.01
guówù yuàn	国务院	22.06
gǔ-jīn-zhōng-wài	古今中外	44.07

H

hāhā	哈哈	02.06
hài ↘	嗐	46.03
hái bùrú	还不如	34.01
hái...ne	还...呢	25.03
hǎiwài guānxi	海外关系	23.11
hái-bù-jiù-nàma-yàng?	还不就那么样？	40.02
hǎn	喊	23.06
hei ⌐	嘿	09.09
heng/hng ↘	哼	41.08
heng/hng ↗	哼	13.06
héshì	合适	37.04
hēzuìle	喝醉了	44.13
hōu	*齁	24.11
huài máobìng	坏毛病	36.12
huàn	换	35.01
huānyíng	欢迎	23.04
huítóu	回头	12.04
hūlu	*呼噜	27.01
húnào	胡闹	27.07
hùnde	混得	46.12
huò	货	27.08
huǒ zàng	火葬	28.14
huódòng	活动	56.01

huǒhou	＊火候	24.05
huópo	活潑	47.16
húshuō	胡説	50.02
hútòng(r)	胡同兒	13.10

J

jǐ	擠	15.05
jià	嫁	38.06
jiācháng fàn	家常飯	24.04
jiàn guó	建國	22.02
jiǎng	講	13.03
jiǎngjiu	講究	36.09
jiāo	交	13.11
jiàoliàn	教練	03.03
jiāxiāng	家鄉	12.01
jiē	接	23.02
jiè zhài	借債	36.15
jiěfu	姐夫	23.01
jiēshi	結實	27.09
jìn	盡	04.09
jingchang	經常	38.04
jíngyàn	經驗	44.12
jiūjìng	究竟	04.07
jiùjiu	舅舅	05.14
jìzhě	記者	19.11
juésài yuán	＊決賽員	58.02
jūnzi-gùqióng,	＊君子固窮，	40.01
xiǎorén-qióng	小人窮斯	
sīlàn yi!	濫矣！	
jǔxíng	舉行	28.13

huǒhou	*火候	24.05
huópo	活泼	47.16
húshuō	胡说	50.02
hútòng(r)	胡同儿	13.10

J

jǐ	挤	15.05
jià	嫁	38.06
jiācháng fàn	家常饭	24.04
jiàn guó	建国	22.02
jiǎng	讲	13.03
jiǎngjiu	讲究	36.09
jiāo	交	13.11
jiàoliàn	教练	03.03
jiāxiāng	家乡	12.01
jiē	接	23.02
jiè zhài	借债	36.15
jiěfu	姐夫	23.01
jiēshi	结实	27.09
jìn	尽	04.09
jīngcháng	经常	38.04
jīngyàn	经验	44.12
jiūjìng	究竟	04.07
jiùjiu	舅舅	05.14
jìzhě	记者	19.11
juésài yuán	*决赛员	58.02
jūnzi-gùqióng,	*君子固穷，	40.01
xiǎorén-qióng	小人穷斯	
sīlàn yǐ!	滥矣！	
jǔxíng	举行	28.13

K

kàn-bu-guàn	看不慣	47.14
kàng	*炕	09.24
kàn-bu-shàng	看不上	40.18
kǎo	烤	28.17
kào...guò rìzi	靠... 過日子	36.14
kǎo-bu-qǔ	考不取	47.23
kě-néng-le	可能了	28.05
kèwén	課文	12.02
kě-kǒu-kě-lè	可口可樂	02.03
kǔ guā	*苦瓜	09.02
kǔ	苦	09.05
kuān	寬	37.10
kuàzhe	挎着	38.05
kùnnán	困難	46.14
kuòjiàn	擴建	22.04
kùzi	褲子	36.32

L

lái-bu-jí	來不及	24.07
láijìng(r)	來勁兒	44.10
láizhe	來着	09.19
lái-de-jí	來得及	51.06
lǎobǎn	老板	36.17
láodòng	勞動	46.16
lǎojiā	老家	23.14
lǎoshì	老式	15.09

K

kàn-bu-guàn	看不惯	47.14
kàng	*炕	09.24
kàn-bu-shàng	看不上	40.18
kǎo	烤	28.17
kào...guò rizi	靠...过日子	36.14
kǎo-bu-qǔ	考不取	47.23
kě-néng-le	可能了	28.05
kèwén	课文	12.02
kě-kǒu-kě-lè	可口可乐	02.03
kǔ guā	*苦瓜	09.02
kǔ	苦	09.05
kuān	宽	37.10
kuàzhe	挎着	38.05
kùnnán	困难	46.14
kuòjiàn	扩建	22.04
kùzi	裤子	36.32

L

lái-bu-jí	来不及	24.07
láijìng(r)	来劲儿	44.10
láizhe	来着	09.19
lái-de-jí	来得及	51.06
lǎobǎn	老板	36.17
láodòng	劳动	46.16
lǎojiā	老家	23.14
lǎoshì	老式	15.09

123

lǎoyé	＊老爺	28.22
lèide huang	累得慌	36.03
liǎ	倆	12.05
lián...dōu	連... 都	40.04
liǎng kǒu	兩口	53.02
liǎng kǒu(r)	兩口兒	25.01
liàozi	料子	46.02
lìhai	厲害	37.15
lǐmào	禮貌	13.04
líng	靈	44.14
lìng jiě	令姐	44.03
lǐngdǎo	領導	36.28
línggōng	零工	01.03
línshí gōng	臨時工	01.04
liúxué	留學	47.24
liúxíng	流行	40.15
liùzhene!	＊溜着呢！	13.13
líxiū	離休	23.12
lòu-yi-shǒu(r)	露一手兒	13.16
luàn	亂	29.03

M

ma	嘛	05.16
mábù dài	＊蔴布袋	46.04
mǎn	滿	28.09
mánzhe	瞞着	41.03
màzha	＊螞蚱	28.10
méi chūxi	沒出息	19.06
méi shàng	沒上	53.04
méi qì(r)	＊沒氣兒	09.10

lǎoye	* 老爷	28.22
lèide huang	累得慌	36.03
liǎ	俩	12.05
lián...dōu	连... 都	40.04
liǎng kǒu	两口	53.02
liǎng kǒu(r)	两口儿	25.01
liàozi	料子	46.02
lìhai	厉害	37.15
lǐmào	礼貌	13.04
líng	灵	44.14
lìng jiě	令姐	44.03
lǐngdǎo	领导	36.28
línggōng	零工	01.03
línshí gōng	临时工	01.04
liúxué	留学	47.24
liúxíng	流行	40.15
liùzhene!	* 溜着呢！	13.13
líxiū	离休	23.12
lòu-yi-shǒu(r)	露一手儿	13.16
luàn	乱	29.03

M

ma	嘛	05.16
mábù dài	* 麻布袋	46.04
mǎn	满	28.09
mánzhe	瞒着	41.03
màzha	* 蚂蚱	28.10
méi chūxi	没出息	19.06
méi shàng	没上	53.04
méi qì(r)	* 没气儿	09.10

méi duì(r)	沒對兒	05.22
méi jìng(r)	＊沒勁兒	04.05
méige-zhèngjing	沒個正經	36.33
méishàng-méixiàde	沒上沒下的	47.17
miànzi	面子	44.06
míng-bǎi-zhe	明擺着	40.09
mō	摸	09.17

N

n/ng ↘	嗯	19.22
ná...lai mēng wǒ	拿...來矇我	41.06
nán chán	難纏	44.11
nào yìjian	鬧意見	36.29
nǎodai	腦袋	47.19
nà-hái-yǒu-cuò (r)?	那還有錯兒？	39.05
nián	粘	28.03
niàn báizì	念白字	19.02
niánqīng	年輕	38.01
niào	＊尿	09.23
ní-měi-de-shénme-ya?	你美的甚麼呀？	40.07
nòng-bu-hǎo	弄不好	47.30
nóngmào shìchǎng	＊農貿市場	51.01

O

o ↗	哦	05.05
o ↘	噢	05.07

méi duì(r)	没对儿	05.22
méi jìng(r)	*没劲儿	04.05
méige-zhèngjīng	没个正经	36.33
méishàng-méixiàde	没上没下的	47.17
miànzi	面子	44.06
míng-bǎi-zhe	明摆着	40.09
mō	摸	09.17

N

n/ng ꜗ	嗯	19.22
ná...lai mēng wǒ	拿...来蒙我	41.06
nán chán	难缠	44.11
nào yìjian	闹意见	36.29
nǎodai	脑袋	47.19
nà-hái-yǒu-cuò (r)?	那还有错儿？	39.05
nián	粘	28.03
niàn báizì	念白字	19.02
niánqīng	年轻	38.01
niào	*尿	09.23
nǐ-měi-de-shénme-ya?	你美的甚么呀？	40.07
nòng-bu-hǎo	弄不好	47.30
nóngmào shìchǎng	*农贸市场	51.01

O

o ꜛ	哦	05.05
o ꜜ	噢	05.07

P

pài	派	19.12
pāo	*泡	28.20
piàoliang	漂亮	37.01
píng	憑	19.18
pútao jiǔ	葡萄酒	24.06

Q

qí yuè fèn	七月份	05.09
qíchē	騎車	32.02
qiàn qián	欠錢	36.11
qián xī	前夕	52.01
qiānwàn	千萬	36.27
qiáo	瞧	05.13
qiāo	敲	47.18
qīn dìdi	親弟弟	36.08
qǐng	請	02.01
Qīngdǎo	青島	05.04
qīngxǐng diǎn(r)	清醒點兒	40.21
qìngzhù	慶祝	60.01
qípáo	旗袍	37.05
qiú	求	15.08
qiúmí	球迷	38.09
quán	全	15.12

R

ràng	讓	05.06
rǎngrang	嚷嚷	46.01

P

pài	派	19.12
pāo	*泡	28.20
piàoliang	漂亮	37.01
píng	凭	19.19
pútao jiǔ	葡萄酒	24.06

Q

qī yuè fèn	七月份	05.09
qíchē	骑车	32.02
qiàn qián	欠钱	36.11
qián xī	前夕	52.01
qiānwàn	千万	36.27
qiáo	瞧	05.13
qiāo	敲	47.18
qīn dìdi	亲弟弟	36.08
qǐng	请	02.01
Qīngdǎo	青岛	05.04
qīngxǐng diǎn(r)	清醒点儿	40.21
qìngzhù	庆祝	60.01
qípáo	旗袍	37.05
qiú	求	15.08
qiúmí	球迷	38.09
quán	全	15.12

R

| ràng | 让 | 05.06 |
| rǎngrang | 嚷嚷 | 46.01 |

rèhe jìn(r)	* 热和劲儿	27.04
rénjiā	人家	47.15
rén-shì-tiě,	* 人是铁，	51.07
fàn-shì-gāng	饭是钢	
rìlì	日历	47.09

S

sài qiú	赛球	58.01
shàng	上	24.10
shāngxīn	伤心	29.04
shāo	烧	28.15
shěde	舍得	47.25
shéi...shéi jiù	谁...谁就	36.10
shēng rén	生人	13.01
shǐ	使	25.02
shìchen	适衬	37.12
shìde	似的	28.02
shìjiè	世界	19.13
shìshi	试试	25.08
shíxīng	时兴	39.03
shízhuāng	时装	30.01
shōu	收	40.10
shǒudū	首都	22.5
shōushí zhuōzi	收拾桌子	50.01
shōushōu xīn	收收心	40.11
shǒuyì	手艺	24.02
shǔ	数	15.14
shū	输	33.06
shuā wǎn	刷碗	15.01
shuǎ píqi	耍脾气	36.24

shuài	帥	13.12
shūfu	舒服	37.16
shuǐ zàng	水葬	28.19
shuì jiào	睡覺	12.03
shuǐpíng	水平	15.10
shuōshuō	說說	36.26
shuō-de-shàng-huà	說得上話	47.05
shūshu	叔叔	09.01
sìhé yuàn	*四合院	28.08
sīrén jiàoshī	*私人教師	04.02
sìxǐ wánzi	四喜丸子	24.01
suàn	算	33.02
suānsuān(r)de	酸酸兒的	44.02
suìshu	歲數	36.23
suōshuǐ	縮水	37.14

T

táizi	檯子	33.01
tǎng xia	躺下	25.07
tàngzhe	燙着	51.03
tāo ěrduo	*掏耳朵	44.15
tǎoyàn	討厭	13.08
tā-māde!	*他媽的！	09.11
tè	特	04.04
téng	疼	19.05
tèyì	特意	39.04
tǐ xiào	*體校	03.02
tiāo	挑	37.02
tiáopí	調皮	05.20
tiàowǔ	跳舞	39.07

shuài	帅	13.12
shūfu	舒服	37.16
shuǐ zàng	水葬	28.19
shuì jiào	睡觉	12.03
shuǐpíng	水平	15.10
shuōshuō	说说	36.26
shuō-de-shàng-huà	说得上话	47.05
shūshu	叔叔	09.01
sìhé yuàn	*四合院	28.08
sīrén jiàoshī	*私人教师	04.02
sìxǐ wánzi	四喜丸子	24.01
suàn	算	33.02
suānsuān(r)de	酸酸儿的	44.02
suìshu	岁数	36.23
suōshuǐ	缩水	37.14

T

táizi	台子	33.01
tǎng xia	躺下	25.07
tàngzhe	烫着	51.03
tāo ěrduo	*掏耳朵	44.15
tǎoyàn	讨厌	13.08
tā-māde!	*他妈的！	09.11
tè	特	04.04
téng	疼	19.05
tèyì	特意	39.04
tǐ xiào	*体校	03.02
tiāo	挑	37.02
tiáopí	调皮	05.20
tiàowǔ	跳舞	39.07

tǐng	挺	19.17
tíxǐng	提醒	40.03
tí-yi-tí	提一提	47.21
tóng bān	同班	13.09
tǒng lóuzi	*捅婁子	05.21
tóng xìng liàn	同性戀	47.29
tū nǎomén(r)	*禿腦門兒	38.08
tuì bù	退步	18.01

W

wán(r)mìng	玩兒命	28.01
wàng hòu	往後	41.01
wàngběn-de-dōngxi	忘本的東西	40.19
wànyī	萬一	47.22
wàzi	襪子	35.03
wèidao	味道	44.01
wǒ-shuō	我說	05.24
wù diǎn	誤點	23.03
wúliáo	無聊	40.14
wǔ-jiǎng-sì-měi	*五講四美	13.02
wǔqī gànxiào	*五七幹校	46.15

X

xī zhǐ	錫紙	28.12
xià lìng	下令	22.07
xià huàile	嚇壞了	05.03
xià	嚇	09.22
xiǎo húzi	小鬍子	38.03
xiǎo-huǒzi	小伙子	38.02

tǐng	挺	19.17
tíxǐng	提醒	40.03
tí-yi-tí	提一提	47.21
tōng bān	同班	13.09
tǒng lóuzi	*捅娄子	05.21
tóng xìng liàn	同性恋	47.29
tū nǎomén(r)	*秃脑门儿	38.08
tuì bù	退步	18.01

W

wán(r)mìng	玩儿命	28.01
wǎng hòu	往后	41.01
wàngběn-de-dōngxi	忘本的东西	40.19
wànyī	万一	47.22
wàzi	袜子	35.03
wèidao	味道	44.01
wǒ-shuō	我说	05.24
wù diǎn	误点	23.03
wúliáo	无聊	40.14
wǔ-jiǎng-sì-měi	*五讲四美	13.02
wǔqī gànxiào	*五七干校	46.15

X

xī zhǐ	锡纸	28.12
xià lìng	下令	22.07
xià huàile	吓坏了	05.03
xià	吓	09.22
xiǎo húzi	小胡子	38.03
xiǎo-huǒzi	小伙子	38.02

xiǎo qǔ(r)	小曲兒	40.16
xiāshuō	瞎説	46.09
xié	鞋	35.02
xiéwèi(r)	*邪味兒	09.14
xiēxie	歇歇	01.06
xiēzhe	*歇着	09.04
xíguàn le	習慣了	36.04
xǐng guolai	醒過來	09.08
xìng guānxi	性關係	47.28
xìng bìng	性病	36.34
xīnkǔ	辛苦	23.05
xīn-lǐ-yǒu-shù(r)	心裡有數兒	37.13
xīn-tiē-xīn	*心貼心	47.6
xiùqi	秀氣	37.09

Y

yáng nǚxu	洋女婿	47.31
yáng wén(r)	洋文兒	41.07
yàngzi	樣子	37.03
yányuan	*言語	15.02
yāo	腰	37.08
yāo	邀	32.01
yàobu	要不	47.11
yàoburán	要不然	37.11
yèyú	業餘	03.01
yì gǔ	一股	09.13
yí bèizi	一輩子	09.06
yìngfu	應付	15.07
yí-hào-rén	一號人	40.22
yo ↗	哟	02.02

130

xiǎo qǔ(r)	小曲儿	40.16
xiāshuō	瞎说	46.09
xié	鞋	35.02
xiéwèi(r)	*邪味儿	09.14
xiēxie	歇歇	01.06
xiēzhe	*歇着	09.04
xíguàn le	习惯了	36.04
xǐng guolai	醒过来	09.08
xìng guānxi	性关系	47.28
xìng bìng	性病	36.34
xīnkǔ	辛苦	23.05
xīn-lǐ-yǒu-shù(r)	心里有数儿	37.13
xīn-tiē-xīn	*心贴心	47.6
xiùqi	秀气	37.09

Y

yáng nǚxu	洋女婿	47.31
yáng wén(r)	洋文儿	41.07
yàngzi	样子	37.03
yányuan	*言语	15.02
yāo	腰	37.08
yāo	邀	32.01
yàobù	要不	47.11
yàoburán	要不然	37.11
yèyú	业余	03.01
yì gǔ	一股	09.13
yí bèizi	一辈子	09.06
yìngfu	应付	15.07
yì-hào-rén	一号人	40.22
yo ↗	哟	02.02

131

Pinyin Transcription of Dialogue

Prepared by Galal Walker
with assistance from
Christine Rodgers, Tang Rong, and Shi Tong

June 1993

East Asian Languages and Literatures
The Ohio State University

Note: This transcription has been prepared directly from the dialogue spoken in the film and contains slight discrepancies from the character script.

A GREAT WALL

(Běijīng de gùshì)

Dìyījié

Dìyīmù---Qù zǎotáng dǎ línggōng

Shīfu:	Xǐzǎo?
Yīdá:	Bù-xǐ.
Shīfu:	Gàn shénmo?
Yīdá:	Línshígōng.
Shīfu:	Lái.
Shīfu:	Èi. Géi nǐ.
Yīdá:	Èi. Nǐ xièxie.

Dìèrmù---Zǎihuá qǐng Yīdá hē kěkǒukělè

Yīdá:	Duōshǎo qián yìpíng(r)?
Xiǎofán:	Qīmáo.
Gùkè:	Yò, tài guì le.
Yīdá:	Zánmen zhè língshígōng yìtiān cái zhèng yíkuàiwǔ a.
Yīdá:	Zhèi shì shénmo ya?
Zǎihuá:	Hehe! Hehe! Hehe!

Dìsānmù---Zài Běihǎi yèyú tǐxiào

Jiàoliàn:	Ē, Kuài!

Dìsìmù--- Xiǎojuān zài jiēshàng pèngjiànle Lìli

Xiǎojuān :	Lìli, Lìli.
Lìli:	Zhāng Xiǎojuān. Shàng nǎr a?
Xiǎojuān :	Zuór nǐ zěnmo méi-qù yīngyǔbān shàngkè a? Lǐbàiyī nǐ yě méiyǒu qù.
Lìli:	Wǒ bàba shuō gěi wǒ zhǎo gè sīrén jiàoshī. Nèi yīngwén bǔxíbān(r) tè méi-jìng.
Xiǎojuān:	Nǐ xiàcì yídìng děi lái bǔxíbān bāng wǒ duìfu duìfu.
Lìli:	Jiūjìng shì něi liǎngge xiǎozi...?
Xiǎojuān:	Jiùshì zuò zài hòumiān(r) shàngkè jìn dǎdǔn(r) de nèige.
Lìli:	Shàngkè dǎdǔn(r) de yǒu hǎo jǐgè ne, shì gāode háishì ǎide?
Xiǎojuān:	Bù-gāo.
Lìli:	Ài, wǒ dào jiā le.
Xiǎojuān:	Ài.
Lìli:	Zàijiàn.
Xiǎojuān:	Zàijiàn.

Dìwǔmù---Zài Zhàojiā

Zhào XS:	Eya, zhè xīn chē jiù zhènmo zāotà. Lìli, jīn(r) nǐ shì zěnmo la. Ōyō, ā, nǐ kàn, bá zhège niǎo, gěiwo, gěi xiàhuài le.
Zhào TT:	Qiáo, Lìlì! Zhèi shì shénmo?
Lìli:	Zánmèn shénmo shíhòu shàng Qīngdǎo a? Shàngcì nín shuōde?
Zhào TT:	O, ràng wǒ kànkàn. O, ānpái de shì qīyuèfèn.
Lìli:	Gāng hǎo shì gāo kǎo nèi yuè. Nà wǒ zěnmo qù a?
Zhào TT:	Yào xiǎng qù Qīngdǎo, jiào nǐ bàba chóngxīn ānpái bú-jìué le. Ou, dùile, nǐ qiáo, nǐ jiùjiu láixìn le. Kàn, kuài kànkan, xiě(de) shénme ya?
Lìli:	*My dearest niece,...*
Zhào TT:	Dàgài shìge shénmo yìsi?
Lìli:	*It has been a long time...*
Zhào TT:	Éi, dàgài shì shénme yìsi? Á?

Lìli: Eiya, nǐ bié cuī ma, wǒ zhè chá(ne) dōu chábúguòlái le ne.

Zhào TT: Nǐ jiùjiu a, chūqù sānshíduō nián le, bā chéng lían Zhōngguozìr dōu bú-huì xiě le. Chūqù de shíhòu gāng shísuì, guǎng tiáopí bú-zhīdao niànshū, kěshì tǒng lóuzi de shì(r) ne méi duì(r).

Lìli: À! Wǒ zuómo chǔlái le. Jiùjiu tāmen jiù yào lái Běijīng.

Zhào TT: Ei, shìa, wǒ shuō, dìdi yòu shuō zhèi huí(r) yào lái le.

Dìèrjié

Dìliùmù--- Zài Měiguó Jiāzhōu yī gāojí zhùzháiqū

Neil: *Oh, that's it! Damn it. I've been trying to debug that program for the whole week. My god!*

Fang XS *I don't know about your god, but my god should be a nice looking Chinese guy which is perfectly circumcised.*

Neil: *Perfectly? !*

Fang XS: *Perfectly.*

Dìqīmù---Zài Fāngjiā

Fang XS: À, níuròu miàn. *Thank you, dear. What do you have to say about your report card, son?*

Baoluo: *Nothing.*

Fang TT: *Professor Chuang just called. He said you only showed up for his Chinese One class once.*

Baoluo: *I have been going to Chinese class ever since I can remember. You know what? I never got to watch Bugs Bunny.*

Fang XS: *Son, nobody should deny his own cultural background. Although we sent you to Chinese school every year, but you still don't speak Chinese!*

Dìjǐumù--- Zài Líujiā de dàzáiyuàn(r)

Zǎihuā:	Shūshu, kǔguā, nǐn chángchang.
Líu XS:	M, kǔ yí bèizi, wǒ bù-chī zhègè.
Zǎihuā:	Yīdá xīezhe ne?
Zǎihuā:	Gē(r)men(r), xǐngguòlái, xíng bu-xíng? Sǐ le? Hei, zhēn méi-qì(r) le, zhèi huí zhei gē(r)men zhēn méi-qì(r) le.
Yīdá:	Tā-māde! Shǒu wǎng nǎr gēlái zhe, māde yìgǔ xiéwèi(r).
Zǎihuā:	Méi wèi(r) a, kàn gē(r)mén(r) zhèi shǒu zhǎngde dūo yǒu fúqì, jiùshi xiǎng mō xiǎng pèng de dōumō bú-zháo gòu bù-shàng ne. Ā, Měiguó xiànzài shéi chànggē zuì yǒumíng a?
Yīdá:	Luciano Pavarotti.
Zǎihuā:	O! Shéi ya? Nǐn shuō gè duǎn de xíng bu-xíng? Shì bu-shì jiùshi chàng nèigè bīnglěng de xiǎo jiǎo(r) de nèige?
Yīdá:	Bīng, bīngliáng de xiǎo shǒu.
Zǎihuā:	Chàng yige! Gē(r)men(r) jiù ài tīng nèige. Chàng yige!
Yīdá:	(Chànggē...)
Línjū:	Bié chàng le! Xià de Sān(r) niào kàng le.

Dìshímù--- Zài Měiguó yíge jiànshēnfáng

Mrs. Fang:	*We've been preparing for a trip to Peking for the last five years. He has a standing invitation from his sister in Peking, and the China Computer Society. I even took him seriously once and took a class in Chinese.*
Woman:	*I thought you spoke Chinese.*
Mrs. Fang:	*Can't you tell? I'm an American!*

Dì Shíyī Mù--- Zài diànnǎo gōngsī

Mr. Fang:	*I don't know about our president, Wilson. He's so indecisive.*

Neil: *Ah, I mean it's only natural. After all, you've been in charge of that PC division for the past four years now.*

Mr. Fang: *I only did the technical part of the project, you have done all this administrative work. Haven't you?*

Neil: *Yeah, well somebody has to mop up the floors. Not that I enjoy it, I was told to do it.*

Mr. Fang: *Hey Jimmy! How ya' doin'?*

Man: *Hey Leo. Congratulations, I heard the word about you becoming the new director of the PC division.*

Mr. Fang: *Thank you.*

Man: *You really deserve it.*

Mr. Fang: *But it hasn't been official yet.*

Dì Shíèr Mù--- Zài mǒu Yīngyǔ bǔxíbān

Lǎoshī: *Today we are going to have new lesson.* Jīntiān, nèige... zánmen yào jiǎng dìèrshíèr kè, *"My Hometown"* Jiùshi *"Wǒde jiāxiāng". Listen to me carefully.* Wǒ xiān bǎ kèwén dú yixia, dàjiā zhùyì tīng a, zhèige, zhùyì tīng de shíhòu, nǐ xiǎngxiǎng Zhōngwén shénmo yìsi, nǐ kàn nǐ néng dǒng duōshǎo. *My hometown is a beautiful place. It stands beside a wide river...*

Zǎihuá: Bié shuìjiào!

Yīdá: Bú-shuì bù-chéng a, zhèi shū wǒ yǐjīng dúgùo sānbiàn le.

Xiǎojuān: Nǐ kàn, tā shùizháole.

Lìli: (xiào)

Zǎihuá: Xiàkè zánmen yídìng gēn tāmen shuōshuōhùa.

Yīdá: Shuō shénmo ya?

Zǎihuá: Jiù shuō jiè bǐjìběn(r) a.

Lǎoshī: Dǒng bù-dǒng a?

Lǎoshī: Nǐmen dǒng bù-dǒng a? *"River"* shénmo yìsī? *"River"*.

Dì Shísān Mù--- Zài jiàoshì wàibiān(r)

Zǎihuá: Nín hǎo!

Lìli: Nǐ hǎo shénmo ya? Yòu bú-shì Měiguorén, jiànle shēngrén hái děi nǐ hǎo nǐ hǎo de.

5

Zǎihuá:	"Wǔ-Jiǎng-Sì-Měi", jiǎng lǐmào a!
Lìli:	Ā, shì bú-shì nǐ?
Zǎihuá:	Bù, bú-shì wǒ.
Lìli:	Bú-shì nǐ, heng, jiù shì nǐ.
Yīdá:	Wǒ,...méi-yǒu a!
Lìli:	Fǎnzhèng nǐmen liǎng, gànmá lǎo xiǎng gōuda Zhāng Xiǎojuān? Tǎoyàn.
Zǎihuá:	Kàn nín shuōde, dōu shì tóngbān tóngxué háiyǒu bù-shuōhuà de?
Lìli:	Shéi shì nǐmen tóngxúe ya? Hútòng(r) lǐ de.
Zǎihuá:	Hútòng(r) lǐ de zěnmo le? Nín bù-yě hútòng lǐ de ma?
Lìli:	Nǐ xiǎng zěnmo yàng?
Zǎihuá:	Jiāo gè péngyou. Wǒmen zhèi gē(r)mén(r) duō shuài, Yīngwén shuōde liùzhe ne, zhèngjing de, hái huì chàng gējù. Gē(r)mèn(r), yě lòuyishǒu(r), nèi jiào shénmo láizhe? "Pápuō(r) luòdǐ"?
Yīdá:	Bù, Pavarotti.

Dìsānjié

Dì Shísì Mù--- Zài diànnǎo gōngsī

Wilson: *Well, Jim has already discussed our income for the year. Keep it up! Gentlemen, and Francis, uh, our PC computer, Compricot, has been very competitive thanks to Leo, Neil, and their fellow workers. It therefore should come as no surprise that we've decided to establish a new PC division. The new director of this PC division is... Mr. Neil Mahoney. And Compricot's inventor, Leo Fang, has been promoted to headquarters as senior member of our technical staff to our senior vice-president.*

Mr. Fang: *Five years ago you told me I didn't have enough experience to be director. Now, Neil Mahoney has less experience than I had five years ago.*

Wilson: *There were other considerations.*

Mr. Fang: *Like what?*

Wilson: *Well, such as youth. I mean Neil's younger than you.*

Mr. Fang: *Oh, so you're telling me I'm too old for this job.*

Wilson: *No, I don't mean that at all. Now look, Neil has lots of good qualities. Now listen to me Leo!*

Mr. Fang: *Neil, Neil doesn't know the system well.*

Wilson: *He'll learn. He'll learn. Look, you have a real good job, very high up in the company, hardly any hassle.*

Mr. Fang: *Let me tell you what I think you're thinking. Let me tell you: You don't believe the Chinaman is good enough to be the director. That's what you're thinking.*

Dì Shíwǔ Mù--- Zài Liújiā dàzáyuàn

Fùnǚ: Xiǎo Sān(r), huílái, shuāle wǎn zài qù kàn diànshì!

Xiǎo Sān(r): Èi, jiù lái.

Zhào XS: Méi-cuò(r), jiùshi zhèi(r). Liú Xiānshēng a, Lǎo Liú Xiānshēng a!

Liú XS: Yō! Lǎo Zhào, nǐ zěnmo lái le? Yě bù-yányü yìshēng, nǐ kàn, zhèi shì duōshǎo nián la!

Zhào XS: Shìa. Wǒ zhè lái qiú nín bāngmáng lái le. Zhèi shì wǒ guīnü.

Liú XS: Eyo, dōu chéng dà rén le ma! Nǐ qiáo. Wūlǐ zuò, wūlǐ zùo. Wǒ zhèi(r) chúqu zāngluàn, jiùshi jǐ diǎn(r).

Zhào XS: Zhe..., wǒ zhèi guīnü a, biéde gōngkè dōu kěyǐ, jiùshi zhèige Yīngyǔ a chà diǎn(r). Zhèbu, dùifu gāokǎo háiyǒu diǎn(r) nán. Qiú nín lái jiāojiao.

Liú XS: Wǒ zhèi Yīngyǔ a, yěshì lǎo shì Yīngyǔ là, zài shuō shuǐpíng yě yǒuxiàn.

Zhào XS: Nǎ(r) a, quán Běijīng shéi bù-zhīdào chúle Xǔ Guózhāng jiù shǔ nín Liú Lǎo Xiānsheng la.

Dì Shíliù Mù--- Zài Liújiā shàngkè

Liú XS: Zhèi shì shénmo shítài? *If you want to study English well, you must study hard. That means memorizing the dictionary. When I was young, I used to memorize fifty words a day.* Zàiwǒ niánqīng de shíhòu, wǒ yītiān yào jìta wǔshígè dānzì. *Even if I forget fourty-five words,* wǒa jiùshi wàngle sìshíwǔ ge, nà wǒ háiyǒu wǔge zì, búshì ma? *But some person doesn't want to do this. I don't know why. Okay, excuse me.*

Dì Shíqī Mù---Zài Fāngjiā kètīng

Paul: *Let's get married. Now.*

Linda: *Your father might come home early.*

Paul: *Pretend he's in China now.*

Linda: *Paul, are you really going to China this summer?*

Paul: *Actually, I don't think we're ever really gonna get there. You know what?*

Linda: *What?*

Paul: *I don't think he really wants to go.*

Linda: *Why not?*

Paul: *'Cause reality often produces disappointments. Funny old man.*

Mr. Fang: *Hey, everybody, I have an announcement to make! I'm gonna have a vacation! One month or even longer. How's that?*

Paul: *Pop, for real?*

Mr. Fang: *You bet. We're all going. You deserve it, I deserve it. We finally deserve it.*

Paul: *You mean like... all four of us? .....Oh.*

Dì Shíbā Mù--- Zài Běihǎi yèyútǐxiào

Lìli: Kěyǐ ma, nǐ xiànzaì qiú dǎ de bú-cuò ma!

Yīdá: Nǎr a! Wǒ zhèi hái tuìbù hǎo dūo le ne.

Dì Shíjiǔ mù--- Zài Yuánmíngyuán fèixū

Lìli: *Bay, B-A-Y.*

Yīdá: Dǎoyǔ.

Lìli: *Yees land.*

Yīdá: Shénmo?

Lìli: *I-S-LAND, iceland.*

Yīdá: No, niàn *island*.

Lìli: Shéi shuō de?

Yīdá: Wǒ bàba. Tā hái néng cuò ma?

Lìli: Zhēn diūrén, niàn dà báizì. Heng, heng. Wǒ kàn nǐ bàba àndì-lǐ tǐng téng nǐ de.

Yīdá: Kě tā lǎo júede wǒ méi-kǎoshàng dàxúe, méi-chūxi. Jiù suàn wǒ kǎoqǔle dà xúe,
           wǒde běnshì hé tā yíyàng dà, yòu zěnmo yàng ne? Hái bú-shì yíyàng zhù dà
           záyuàn(r)? Ā, tīng wǒde.

           *"Four score and seven years ago, our fathers...brought forth on this continent a new
           nation, a new nation considered in levity and dedicated to the proposition that all
           men are created equal. We here highly **resort** that this nation under God shall have
           not new spurts of freedom and that government of the people, by the people, for the
           people should noot perish from the eeearth."*

Lìli: He, he, he.

Yīdá: Wǒ nèi gāngcái niànde (nèi) dúbái zěnmo yàng?

Lìli: Tǐng hǎo.

Yīdá: Tīngle yǒu méi-yǒu zǒngtǒng de gǎnjué?

Lìli: Dāng jìzhě dāngrán hǎo a, kěyǐ pài dào shìjiè gèdì dàochù guàng, guàng wán le zài
           xiě jǐpiàn gǎnxiǎng. Rénjiā hái gěi dēngchūlái.

Yīdá: Xiǎngde tǐng měi, rénjiā píng shénmo zhuān sòng nǐ qù shìjiè gèdì ya?

Lìli: Bú-sòng wǒ, sòng shéi?

Yídá: Nǐ shuō de duì.

Lìli: Nǐ ne? Nǐ xiǎng gàn shénmo?

Yídá: Wǒ, gàn shénmo dōu kěyǐ, zhǐ yào néng shàngge dàxúe, jiānglái yǒuge hǎo dānwèi, zài fēnshàng wǒme yítạo gōngfáng jiù kěyǐ le.

Lìli: Ng.

Dì Èrshí Mù--- Zài Fāngjiā kètīng

Linda: *Um, I'm leaving. Hi, Mr. Fang, have a pleasant trip.*

Mr. Fang: *Bye, Linda. ...What's wrong, Romeo?*

Paul: *Father, give me a break. Who's playing?*

Mr. Fang: *Forty-niners against Broncos. Hey, I thought you'd stop seeing Linda.*

Paul: *I will... when I'm in China.*

Mr. Fang: *What ever happened to that nice Chinese girl, Margaret Wei?*

Paul: *She's going out with some white guy. You know ... Why don't you like Linda as my friend? You know the only reason you don't like her is 'cause she's not Chinese.*

Mr. Fang: *C'mon, I never suggested anything like that.*

Paul: It's true. All Chinese parents are racist.

Mr. Fang: What are you talking about? Hey!

Paul: You use the tradition and the culture to cover up the racism. Really. Why do we have to do everything the Chinese way anyway? It gets you nowhere. This is America, you know? You've lived here for so long, and you still talk with an accent.

Mr. Fang: What's wrong with my accent? I think it's rather cute.

Mr. Fang: Yes, yes! Sack him!

Mrs. Fang : What's the weight limit on each suitcase again?

Mr. Fang: Forty-four pounds...

Dì Èrshíyī Mù--- Zài Fāngjiā wòfáng

Mrs. Fang: Here's an interesting paragraph about the city of Peking. Listen, "Peking is a city..."

Mr. Fang: Peking is a city surrounded by walls, big thick walls.

Mrs. Fang: What? Why?

Mr. Fang : To keep the invaders out or to confine the natives in. It is just as difficult to leave the city as it is to go back.

Mrs. Fang: What does your sister say in the letter?

Mr. Fang: *Oh, they still didn't do anything about father's grave.*

Mrs. Fang: *Oh no.*

Dì Èrshíèr Mù---Zài Běijīng chénglǐ

Mr. Fang: *Where's the wall?*

Mrs. Fang: *"The Great Wall is located sixty miles northwest of the city...*

Mr. Fang: *I don't mean that wall.* Tóngzhì, Běijīng de chéngqiáng nǎ(r) qù le?

Sījī: O, Běijīng de chéngqiáng a, jiànguó chūqī, wèile kuòjiàn shǒudū Běijīng, bèi guówùyuàn xiàlìng chāichú le.

Mrs. Fāng: *"The wall of Peking city was torn down right after liberation for the purpose of expanding the nation's capital."*

Mr. Fāng: *Geez, what do you know? China expert, eh?*

Mrs. Fāng: *The guidebook doesn't lie all the time.*

Mr. Fāng : *Those damn highrises.*

Dìsìjié
Dì Èrshísān Mù---Zài Zhàojiā Dàménkǒu(r)

Lìli: Mā, bàba, láile! Kuài diǎn(r)!

Fāng XS: Jiě!

Zhào TT: Lìqún ba! A, a, a, o! Zhèi jiùshì nǐ jiěfu.

Fāng XS: Ei, Jiěfu.

Zhào XS: Zuótiān qù fēijīchǎng jiēle nǐmen yìtiān, zěnmo jīntiān cái dào a?

Fāng XS: Fēijī wù diǎn, méi-bànfǎ.

Zhào TT: Ei, nǐ hǎo, nǐ hǎo, huānyíng nǐ. Xīnkǔ le ba?

Fāng *TT:*   *Leo has told me all about you.*

Zhào TT: Lìli, kuài hǎn jiùjiu!

Fāng XS: Lìli, nǐ **hǎo**. Hei, zhèigè(r)!

Zhào XS: Huānyíng nín.

Zhào TT: Lái, nǐ hǎo. Zhèi shì nǐ gūfu.

Línj ūA: Zhèi bāngrén nǎr de ya?

Línjū B: Shì xiǎo Rìběn ba?

Línjū A: Bú-xiàng. Fēilǜbīn rén ba?

Linjū B: Yě bú-xiàng.

Fāng XS: Zhèi yuànzi gēn zánmen lǎojiā yíyàng ma?

Zhào TT: Wánquán bù-yīyàng.

Dì Èrshísì Mù--- Zài Zhàojiā fàntīng chīfàn

duan yirvan cìxǐwánzi

Zhào TT: Lái, lái, lái, chángchang wǒde sìxǐ wánzi.

Fāng XS: Jiě, nǐde shǒuyì kuài gǎnshang māde le.

Zhào TT: Hài, jiācháng fàn, jiācháng fàn. Chángchang. *he*

Zhào XS: Nǐ zhège huǒhòu Hái chà yìdiǎn(r).   *báiqiu hen qiáng=*
                                                     strong

Zhào TT: Shì ma? Lìli, qù bǎ nàge pútao jiǔ nálái!

Lìli: À.

Zhào TT: Wǒ bù-néng hē bái de.

Zhào XS: Dìmèi de shǒuyì bú-cuò ba?

Fāng XS: He's asking about your cooking. Chinese cooking.

Fāng TT: Oh, I only know how to cook beef noodles. Niúròu miàn.

Zhào XS: Ò... niúroù miàn zuò hǎo le, kě bú-yì a! Běijīng a, hái zhēn méi jǐjiā hǎo niúròu miàn guǎnzi lei.

Zhào TT: A, hē, hē, kuài hē!

Bǎoluó: What do you do for fun at school? For fun.

15

v ta buhao yisi

Lìli:　　　Jiùjiu, wǒ zěnmo xúele hǎo jǐnián Yīngyǔ háishi tīng bù-dǒng a?

Fāng XS:　Nǐmen zài xúexiào wán shénmo?

Lìli:　　　Wán(r)? Wǒmen bù-wán(r), wǒmen yǒu shíjiān hái láibùjí xuéxí ne.

Bǎoluó:　　*Do you play sports?*

sports or movement

Lìli:　　　*Sports?* Oh, yùndòng, wǒ xǐhuān dǎ pīngpāng qiú. *I play ping-pong.*

Bǎoluó:　　*No kidding! This is great! That used to be my sport.*

Zhào TT:　Háiyou yītiáo yú, yīguō tāng ne.

Fāng XS:　Chībuliǎo, bié shàng le.

hotel
v

Zhào TT:　Xiǎo dì, dàole Běijīng la nǐ jiù bié zhù lǚguǎn le, hōu guìde, dǎ jīn(r) qǐ a, dōu gěi wǒ bāndào jiālǐ lái zhù, a.

prepare

Zhào XS:　Jiùshi ma! Dōu zhǔnbèi hǎo la, zhǔnbèi hǎo la.

Fāng XS:　*Do you wanna move in? It's all prepared.*

Dì Èrshíwǔ Mù---Zhàoxiānsheng Zhàotàitai zài wòfáng

Zhào XS:　Nǐ dìdi yījiā sānkǒu, liǎngkǒu(r) bú-huì shuō Zhōngguóhuà, kě huì shǐ kuàizi.

Zhào TT:　Nǐ hái bú-huì shǐ dāo chā ne.

Zhào XS:　A, nǐ zhè gǔdao shénmo ne?

Zhào TT: Dìdi sòng gěi zánmen de diàntǎn.

electric blanket

Zhào XS: Diàntǎn, lái, nǐ tǎng xià, wǒ gěi chāshàng diànmén. Lái, lái, shìshi...

Zhào TT: Wǒ cái bú-shì ne.

Zhào XS: Nǐ bú-shì, wǒ shì.

Dì Èrshíliù Mù--- Fāngjiā zài wòfángli

Fang TT: *Leo, do you think they like me?*

bùānquán gǎn = insecure feeling

Fang XS: *Sure, they're crazy about you. Believe me.*

Fang TT: *I feel like I've known them for a long time.*

Fang XS: *Of course. You all belonged to the same herd of cattle in your previous life.*

herd of
yìqún niú = cow

Baoluo: *Dad? They don't have a shower bath here.*

Fang XS: *Too bad.*

Fang TT: *Are you warm enough Paul?*

zhongguo shi de matong

Baoluo: *Are you kidding? I'm hot. They have squat toilets, I don't think I've quite developed the leg muscles for it.*

Fang XS: *You need practice. Oh, shut up. Go to sleep will ya'?*

Dì Èrshíqī Mù--- Zhàotàitai Zhàoxiānsheng zài wòfáng

Zhào XS: Zhèi, Měiguórén jiù zhèimo shuìjiào a? Zhè diàn zài shēnshàng hūlu, hūlu zhí zhuàn, bù-zěnmo nuǎnhuo ma, aha, rèhe jìn(r) shànglái le, hei! Ng? Shénmo wèi(r) a?

Zhào TT: Nǐ zhèi húnào shénmo ya?

Zhào XS: Aya, zhèi Měiguó huò, yě bù-jiēshi a! Dùile, zhǔnshi nǐ dìdi ga ǎo cuòle. Zámen zher diànyā hé tāme nàr bù-yíyàng(r).

not sturdy [handwritten annotation]

Zhào TT: Rénjiā shì měiguóde diànnǎo zhuānjiā, hái bù-dǒng zhèige.

computer expert [handwritten annotation]

Dìwǔjié
Dì Èrshíbā Mù--- Zài Zhāojiā yuànzili

bào fēng yǔ - violent wind rain [handwritten annotation]
dǎ léi = to thunder [handwritten annotation]

Lìli: Jiùjiu.

Fāng XS: Lìli, hái bù-xiēzhe? Zènmo niànshū de ma, wán(r)mìng shì de, wǒ kàn nǐ.

Lìli: Méi-guānxi, fǎnzhèng shùibùzháo.

cicadas [handwritten annotation]

Fāng XS: Nǐ huì nián "zhīliǎo" ma?

Lìli: Wǒ xiǎo shíhòu wǎn(r) guò, bú-guò nèi yìbān dōu shì nán háizi wǎn(r) de.

Fāng XS: Nǎr a? Kàn nǐ mā xiǎo de shíhòu kěnéng le. Nàge dà zhú gān, yǒu tā sānge rén nàme gāo, wàng shùshàng yìchūo jiù yíge. Tā méi-gàosuguo nǐ a?

Lìli: Méi-yǒu.

Fāng XS: Nà shíhòu wǒmen zhùzai hǎo dàde hǎo dàde yíge sìhé yuán(r), mǎn yuànzi dōushì màzha, wǒmen méi-shì(r) jiù bǎ màzha dǎilái, yòng xīzhǐ bāoshàng jǔxíng "huǒ zàng", shāochū nèi wéi(r) gēn kǎo cán dòu shì de, dōu shì nǐ mā xiǎngchūlái de. Bú-guò wǒ yě fāmíng le yíge, wǒ fāmíng nèige jiào "shuǐ zàng"--bǎ nèi màzha

yēncì = drown

nánguò = sad
angry

dāizhe, yìpāo niǎo yìzī, jiù bǎ tā zīsī le. Nǐ lǎoye nà shíhòu yí shēngqì, jiù zuò zài nèige dà shù dǐxià chàng dàgǔ, nántīng jíle.

Dì Èrshíjiǔ Mù--- Zài Fāngjiā féndì

mùdì = graveyard   fénmù = grave

Zhào TT: Wǒmen hǎoxiē rìzi méi-lái le. Bàba guòqù de neìnián, zhèng gǎnshang luàn, yě méi-gěi tā hǎohao de bàn.

wénge = cultural revolution

Fāng XS: Bié shuō le, bié shuō le, jiě.

zhīshi fènzi = intellectuals
dùn xia = squat down

Fāng XS: Son, come here. This is the old man I told you about. He's funnier than you and I put together. Funny man.

hen hǎo xiao = very funny   yīshu huà = bouquet
hen you qù = fun.   yīdou huà = one flower

Dì Sānshí Mù--- Zài shízhuāng biǎoyǎn xùnliàn bān

biǎo xiàn = performance

bu gou gāo = not tall enough

Zǎihuá: Nín sīxiang jiànkang zuòfēng zhèngpai, zánne quán hégé(r). Yaò tā bú-yaò wǒ ya? Zhǐ yǒu gāo gè(r) chuān shízhuāng, aǐ gè(r) jiù bù-chuān le ma? Yīdá, zǒu a!

tāde biǎoxiàn bù hǎo
yidá shi hen xiàng yangzi = as one should, resemble the model

Dì Sānshíyī Mù--- Zǎochén zài Zhàojiā yuànzi zuò yùndòng

Dì Sānshíèr Mù--- Zài Lìli de wòfáng

Zhào TT: Lìli, bié fēng. Zhāng Xiǎojuān gěi nǐ de xìn, nuo, yào nǐmen yìqǐ qíchē qù Yuánmíngyuán. Xúexiào ràng nǐ **a** qù liàn pīngpāng qiú ne. Zhè Xiǎo Qín de xìng. Ai, dài nǐ biǎogē chūqù wán(r)!

Bǎoluó: I can't believe this! Look at this.

Lìli: Zhèi yǒu shénmo a?

Bǎoluó: She reads all your mail!

kan tade xin

19

Lìli: Zhèi yǒu shénmo a?

Bǎoluó: *Haven't you ever heard of a thing called "privacy"?*

Lìli: *Privacy?*

Bǎoluó: *Privacy.*

Bǎoluó: *Yeah, Alright. I guess there's no such thing in China.*

Dì Sān-shí-sān Mù--- Zài Běibǎi yèyútǐxiào   *zài tǐxiào*

coach   *your hand can't touch the table*

Jiàoliàn: Zhèi shǒu a bù-néng fú táizi, yí fú táizi gūizé shì gūidìng jiù suàn fàn guī. Nǐ bù-guǎn nǐ dǎzháo méi dǎzháo dōu suàn nǐ shū, a. Zhùyì diǎn(r) a!

Bǎoluó: (Shǒu yòu pèng táizi)

Jiàoliàn: Zěnmo huíshì a? Gāng gēn nǐ shuōwán le, zhèiyàng, jiàoliàn zěnmo jiào nǐ? a?

Bǎoluó: (Diǎn tóu, biǎoshì zhīdào le)

Dì Sānshìsì Mù--- Zài Chángchéng shàng

Lìli: Jiùjiu, nǐ hái bù-rú wǒmen zǒude kuài ne. Xiǎojuān, kuài lái!   *jìniàn pǐn = souvenir*

Bǎoluó: *What do you think? "Put the Great Wall on your chest."*

Zǎihuá: "Shuō shénme ne?

Bǎoluó: *I'll buy it.*

Fāng XS: *The Great Wall was built thousands of years ago to prevent invaders from the north.*

Fāng TT: *It didn't work.*

Fāng XS: *No, the invaders came from the south.*

kan fengjin=

Dì Sānshíwǔ Mù--- Cānguān mǒu diànzǐ yánjiūsuǒ

shang lou = walk up stairs
pá lóutī = climp stairs

Zǒng GS: Fāng Jiàoshòu, qǐng huànle yīfu.

chuān waiton = put on jacket

Fāng XS: Jīn(r) ge zuò dàifu le, a.

baolù nimen de dianno
baolu dianno = protect computers

Zǒng GS: Fāng Jiàoshòu, qǐng huàn yíxià xié.

Fāng XS: Wàzi yǒuge dòng.   *wàzi pòle = change hole in socks*

Zǒng GS: Qǐng nín zìjǐ shìyíshi ba.

dài shoutuo = wear gloves

Fāng XS: Ah, this character is wrong.

ta bù renshi jiántǐzi = doesn't know simplified

Zǒng GS: No, this is only simplified version.

fántǐzi = traditional

Dìliùjié

Dì Sānshíliù Mù--- Wǎnshàng zài Zhàojiā Liáotiānr

Zhào XS: Zhèi jǐshí nián nǐ chéngtiān jìn shuō zhège wàiguóhùa, zhè zuǐba bú-lèide huāng ma?

Fāng XS: Jiǔle jiù xíguàn le, bù-juéde le.

Fāng TT: *He speaks Chinese all the time, with his relatives and his Chinese friends in the States.*

Zhào TT: Xiǎodì, nǐmen zài wàitou yíge yuè zhèng duōshǎo qián na?

Zhào XS: Hài, kàn nǐ, wèn zhèige, rénjiā Měiguó bù-xīng wèn zhèige.

Zhào TT: Nǐ yòu zhīdào le, chěng shénmo néng a, zhèi wèn zìgě(r) qīn dìdi yǒu shénmo bù-xíng de?

zhèng = earn

Fāng TT: *He earns zero dollars now.* bù zhèng qián. bù méi-you gōngzuò

dàiye zhōngnián = unemployed

Fāng XS: Zài Měiguó a, zhèng duōshǎo qián dōu yíyàng, fǎnzhèng bú-gòu huā de, zài nàr a, jiǎngjiu a shéi qiàn qián duō, shéi jiù yǒu běnshì.

Zhào TT: Yō, nà qiānwàn bié xué zhè huài máobìng. Diē bú-shì cháng shuō ma, zánmen bù-néng kào jiè zhài guò rìzi.

working

Zhào XS: Nǐ xiànzài gēn nèige dānwèi a?

Fāng XS: Wǒ xiànzài méi dānwèi.

Zhào TT: Rénjiā nàr bù-xīng shuō dānwèi. Nǐ nèi jiā gōngsī jiào shénmo láizhe?

Fāng XS: Gōngsī yě méi le. Lín lái de shíhòu gēn lǎobǎn nàofān le. Wǒ xiànzài shì ge dà-xián-rén. Dàiyè zhōngnián, ànzhào nǐmen nàr de huà shuō.

unemployed

act up

Zhào TT: Zhēnde? Dōu zhènmo dà suìshu le, hái shuǎ píqi, nèi zěnmo déliǎo a? Zhǎorén shuōshuo shuōshuo, qiānwàn bié gēn lǐngdǎo nào yìjiàn, tīngjiànle méiyǒu?

Fāng XS: Láibùjí le. Lín zǒu de shíhòu wǒ gēn nà lǎobǎn dàchǎo yíjià, ránhòu wǒ bǎ yìbēi rè kāfēi dào zài tā kùzi shàng le.

argue

Fāng TT: *That was a cup of hot coffee, very hot.*

Zhào TT: Zěnmo dé liǎo ya! Dōu zènmo dà suìshu le, hái méi ge zhèngjīng.

Zhào XS: Tīngshuō zhèi Měiguó chābùduō měige rén dōu dé zhège xìngbìng, shì zhēn de?

V.D.

Fāng XS: *Hee, hee, ha, herpes maybe!*

Fāng TT: *Leo! What are you talking about?*

Dì Sānshíqī Mù--- Zài Zhàojiā

Zhào TT: Nǐ kàn zhèi bù duó piàoliàng. Lái, shìshi.

liáng = measure   bù liǎo = cloth

Fāng TT: *Oh, Chinese fabrics are so beautiful. Too bad they don't pay more attention to fashion design.*

shi mǎo shiji = fashion design
shízhuāng - fashionable clothing

Zhào TT: Zhèige ya, zuò shàng yīfu zuì piàoliàng. Lái, lái, lái, tiāo ge yàngzi. Zhèige bù-hǎo. Zhèige yīfu tài duǎn.

Fāng TT: *Too short.*

Zhào TT: Ai, zhèi yīfu héshì, nǐkàn, qípáo. Ná zhèige bù a, zuò qípáo zuì piàoliàng le. Hǎo rén dōu zènmo zuò de.

Fāng TT: *Don't you think it's too long? Too long?*

Zhào TT: O, bù-cháng, zhèi qípáo jiù děi yào zhènmo cháng, duǎn dào zhèr jiù bù-hǎo kàn le. Jiù zuò zhèige, a.

yào = waist

bù héshēn = can't fit

Fāng TT: *I don't think I could fit into this!*

Zhào TT: Bùkuān, nǐ yǐhòu lǐtóu hái děi chuān yīfu ne. O, dìmèi de yāo zhēn gòu xiùqi de.

Fāng TT: *I am too old for a maternity dress!*

yùnfu = maternity dress

huái yùn = get pregnant

Zhào TT: Shàngmiàn zhèmo dà, xiàmiàn jiù děi zhèmo kuān, yào bù-rán tā bù shíchèn, bù-hǎo kàn. Wǒ xīnlǐ yǒu shù(r). Hǎo, wǒ zhèi huǐ(r) jiù gěi nǐ zuò.

Fāng TT: *Oh, you're going to sew it.*

fēng = to sew

cái fēngjī = sewing machine

Zhào TT: Nǐ kàn a, zhèige bù suōshuǐ tǐng lìhai de. Wǒ xǐle, kěnéng suō le duōshǎo.

Zhào TT: Zhōngguó yīfu a, chuānzài shēnshàng jiù shì shūfu.

Fāng TT: *Oh! It's too big. I haven't been this big since I had Paul!*

Zhào TT: Duō héshì a!

Dìqījié

Dì Sānshíbā Mù--- Zài Zhào tàitai wòfáng huàzhuāng

huàzhuāng v/n = makeup

huàzhuāng pǐn = cosmetics

Zhào TT: O, lǎo le. Nǐ qiáo zhèi zhòuwén(r). Wǒ niánqīng de shíhòu a, xiǎo de shíhòu a, yìxie ge xiǎo huǒzi, dàizhe húzi, hái jīngcháng kuàzhe.

kǒuhóng = lipstick

cā = to apply

Fāng TT: *Oh, you had a lot of guys.*

zhòuwén = wrinkles

jìngzi = mirror

jìngzi hú = mirror lake

24

zhāngfu

Zhào TT: Wǒ méi jià, jià zèmege lǎotóu(r), yòu ǎi, yòu pàng, dùzi yòu dà, háishí tū nǎomén(r), zùi táoyàn de, méi shì(r) hái nòngge jiǔ.

Ta kan dianshǐ eiqie

Fāng TT: Leo, dìdi. *Weekend, He watches TV all weekend. He watches football.*

Zhào TT: *TV, football.*

máiyuàn = complain
tamen xiansheng bu hao

Fāng TT: *Go! Go! Doesn't pay any attention to me.*

Zhào TT: Qiúmí. Dōu yíyàng. Zhèi lǎotóu(r), yì dǎkāi nà diànshì, jiù...

Lìli: Mā.

Ta juede bu hao yisi = tai lǎo le.

Zhào TT: À, shénmo shì(r) a? *bu zhoangtong*

ta jiehun le.

Dì Sānshíjiǔ Mù--- Zài Zhàojiā zhǔnbèi qù sānjiā wǔhuì

Lìli: *Who is Linda?*

shutou ta = comb   *shuzi = a comb*
shua = brush
shuazi = a brush   *you hen dōu pengyu*

Fāng TT: *Oh, she's just one of Paul's friends. Paul has many friends. He's very popular.*

bǎng = to tie

Xiǎojuān: Biédòng, wǒ qù ná yīfu.

bǎng daizi = to tie a ribbon

Fāng TT → bǎng daizi

Zhào TT: Tāmen dōu dǎban hǎo le, wǒmen yě qù dǎonong, dǎonong

zhēnu zhū = pearls

Xiǎojuān: Zhèi shì měiguó zùi shíxīng de ma?

zui shí xīng = latest style

Lìli: Nà hái yǒu cuò(r). Wǒ jiùmā tèyì gěi wǒ mǎi de.

chunzi = dress

Xiǎojuān: Nǐ shìshi.

Lìli:　　　Nǐ juéde zěnmo yàng?

xījuang = suit

Xiǎojuān:　Fēicháng piàoliang.

mà = to scold

zuì yida de ma ta

Lìli:　　　Zhèr hǎoxiàng yòu sōng yòu dà.

Xiǎojuān:　Zhèi shì gěi Měiguó rén chuān de ma.

Yīdá:　　　Xiǎo Yú, guòlái!

Tamen chuan xijuang

Yīdá:　　　Nǐ xiǎozi zhēngòu péngyou. *zhengli yitiao lingdai =*

straighten his tie

Lìli:　　　Yīdá, yíkuài(r) qù tiàowǔ hǎo ma? Zǒu ba! *Tamen qu Yézonghui =*

Zhào TT:　Zǒuba, zǒuba, yǐjìng wǎn le, hái mócèng bàntiān. *Yida bu gaoxing yinwei tamen*

mei xingcha qu.

sign say "huanying" 　　　　　　　*tiaowu = dance*

Dì Sìshí Mù --- Zài Liújiā

neiqeeyéjia 　　　　　*nihong dēng = neon light*

da gu = drumming 　　*xiguang dēng = flouresant lights*

Liú XS:　　"Jūnzi gù qióng, xiǎorén qióng sī làn yi!" Zěnmo, zhèicì zhǔnbèi de zěnmoyàng le?

jù sàng = depressed 　　　　　*dai*

　　　　　　　　　　　　　　　　heiyenjing = anatars,

Yīdá:　　　Hái bù jiù nèmo yàng. 　　　　　　*sunglasses*

　　　　　　　　　　　　　　ta juede hěn coo =

kao bu shang = to fail 　　　*He thinks he's cool*

Liú XS:　　Zhèi shì shénmo huà ne, wǒ zhèshi tíxǐng nǐ! Nǐ zhèi dōu shì dì sāncì cānjiā gāokǎo
　　　　　le, nǐ yàoshì zài kǎobúshàng de huà... 　　*zhulebu = club*

　　　　　　　　　　　　　　　　　yezonghui = niyntclub

Yīdá:　　　Zài kǎobúshàng de huà, wǒ jiù bú-shì rén le. 　*pai sho = clap hands*

Liú XS:　　Wǒ lián dūcù nǐ zhǔnbèi gōngkè dōu bù-chéng le? Nǐ měi shénmo ya? Nǐ! Nǐ
　　　　　dàxué kǎobúshàng dàxúe hái yǒu shénmo chūlù? Zhèi bú-shì míng-bǎi-zhe de
　　　　　ma!

měi you qianqu = have to future

26

Yīdá: Yǒu dàxúe wǒ gànma bú-shàng a! Kě yìnián zhǐzhāo jǐge? Wǒ yǒu shénmo bànfǎ.

liúxíng gē = pop songs

Liú XS: Shōushou-xīn, zhuājǐn shíjiān, zhèihúi yǒu xīwàng. Nǐ qùnián bú jiù chà shíèrfēn mo. Bú-yào gǎo nèixiē wúliáo de shìqing le, dǎ pīngpāng a, chàng liúxíng xiǎo-qǔ(r) le.

wǔ rǔ = to insult   *pìlìyǔ = breakdance*

Yīdá: <u>Dú-sǐ-shū.</u>

kànbuqǐ = look down on, disrespect   *yùdùi = music band*

Liú XS: Nǐ shūo shénmo? Nǐ kànbúshàng nǐ bàba dú-sǐ-shū a? Nǐ yòu hùi shénmo? Wàng-běn-de dōngxi. Měitiān zuòmèng dōu xiǎngzhe gēn Zhào jiā gūniang tán liànaài, gǎode diānhūn dànsì de. Qīngxǐng diǎn(r) ba, Zhào jiā gēn zánmen bú-shì yí-hào-rén.

bashì bǎo dǎi = dnt recognize good from bad. ungrateful

wàng běn = forget oneself

Dìbājié

〜〜〜〜〜

Dì Sì-shí-yī Mù--- Zài Lìli de wòfáng

Zhào TT: A, Yìdá jìgěi nǐde xìn. Tā shūo ya...

Lìli: Mā, wǎng hòu nín biè chāi wǒ de xìn le.

Zhào TT: Shénmo?

Lìli: Chāi kàn biéren de xìn bù-hǎo.

other ppl

Zhào TT: "Biéren"! Nǐ yòu bú-shì "biéren", nǐ shì wǒ nǚ'ér.

Lìli: Nà yě bù-hǎo.

Zhào TT: Zěnmo? Nǐ gànle shénmo huài shì le? Lián nǐ mā dōu mánzhe?

conceal

Lìli: Wǒ méi mánzhe. *privacy.*

privacy

27

máodùn = contradiction

Zhào TT: Á?

Lìli: *privacy* jiùshi *privacy*, bù-néng fānyì. Jiùjiu shuōde.

yīnsī(quán) = privacy - the right toprivacy

to grow wings

Zhào TT: Zhǎng chìbǎng le. Xiànzài jìn ná yáng wén(r) lái mēng wǒ. Nǐ yě bù-xiǎngxiang, méiyǒu nǐ māma, nǎr lái de nǐ! Hèng!

jia jing bao li = domestic violence

Dì Sìshíèr Mù--- Běijīng zǎoshàng de gōngyuán

Dì Sìshísān Mù--- Bǎoluó Lìli gǎn gōnggòngqìzhē

Dì Sìshísì Mù--- Zào xiānsheng Fāngxiānsheng zài fànguǎnr

lóng zi you niǎo = cage w/ bird

gonggong chichi zài gōngyuan chǎojià = verbal argument la èrhú = playing the instrument èrhú

Zhào XS: Weìdào zěnmo yàng?

zai shang ché = getting on bus méi shang ché = to miss the bus shàng buliao sour

Fāng XS: Gòu suānde.

yuèqi = instrument

Bǎoluó: *Dad...money...*

gen zhe che pǎo de houmian pao run for the bus fēn shuo = to break up w/ yida gen lili fen shuo de.

Fāng XS: *Running out again?*

qian kuai hua guan le: run out of money.

yong ji = crowded you ren tai duo

Zhào XS: Nín nèiwèi lìng jiě a, yàngyàng dōu hǎo, jiùshi aì cī(r) rén, dāngzhe háizi de miàn(r), kèrén de miàn(r) yě cī(r), yìdiǎn(r) miànzi yě bù-gěi. A, nǐmen nèiwèi zěnmo yàng?

zunjing zhang bei = respect your elders bu gei ta mianzi = doesnt give him face

Fāng XS: Yíyàng. Gǔ-jīn-zhōng-wài dōu yíyàng.

Zhào XS: Tāmen shuō, zhèige nǚrén dàole gēngniánqī, zhèi huà ya, hěn-nán-shuō, cùjìngr tèbié dà. À, wǒ zènmo dà suìshùle, háinéng zěnmoyàng ne? Zhēnshì.

Fāng XS: Nèi yě shuō bú-dìng a, jiěfu! Gēngnián qī shàng, O, *menopause* zài wàiguó yě yǒu zhèizhǒng shuōfǎ. Zhèi nǚrén yíjìnrù zhèige *menopause* tèbié láijìng na. Hěn nán chán a, huódòng néng lì tèqiáng, érqiě *sexually very active* bú-guò wǒ méi jīngyàn. Wǒ zhèi shì tīng rén shuō de.

Zhào XS: Shì a!   ~~krazaan~~ *(he zuì jiǔ le = drunk)*

Fāng XS: Nǎr wū(r)? Běi wū(r).

(zǒude bù wěn = unstable walking)

Zhào XS: Lái, lái, shàng běi wū. Nǎ shì běi a? Zhèi biān shì běi.

Fāng XS: Zǒu, zǒu, shàng běi fáng, běi wū.

(wǎng běi zǒu)

Zhào XS: Shàng běi fáng? Nǎ(r) shì běi a? Zhèi biān(r). Nǐ a, hēzuìle.

Fāng XS: Méi-zuì.   *(dǎge = to burp)*

Zhào XS: Zhèi shì běi wū.

Fāng XS: *Ah, music!*

Zhào XS: Shìshi, zhèige zuì líng le.

Fāng XS: Ai, bù, bù.

(è xīn = disgusting)

Zhào XS: Nǐ yaò shì zuì a, ...

Fāng XS: Méi-zuì.   *(ěrshǐ = earwax)*

Zhào XS: Nǐ zuì le jiù tāo bù-chéng ěrduo. Zhèi diǎn(r) zú yǒu bànjīn. Kàn nǐde.

(tāo ěrduo = pick ur ear)

Fāng XS: Wǒ lái ma? Méi-wèntí.

Dì Sìshíwǔ Mù--- Zài mǒu qǔyìbiǎoyǎnchǎng tīng Jīngyùntàgǔ

(dǎgu = to drum)

29

(Chàng Cí)

Hànmò zhūhóu luàn fēn zhēng, qún xióng sì qǐ dòng dāo bīng, Cáo Mèngdé wèi yā qún chén quánshì zhòng, xiéchí tiānzǐ bǎ lìng xíng. Dòu zhǐ wèi yào nà Líu Biǎo lái guīshùn, yào qǐng yí wèi fēngliú míngshì qián wǎng shūtōng. Nà Kǒng Róng àizhòng rúshēng lián cáizǐ, xiū bèn shàng biǎo yaò bǎojiàn Mí Héng...

Dì Sìshíliù Mù--- Zǎochén zài Liújiā yuànzi

Lìli: *Paul*, zhèi yíjù shénmo yìsi?

yáogǔn yīnyuè = rock n' roll music

Zhào XS: Dà qīng zǎo(r) de chǎo shénmo a? Ài, chē yě bù-zhīdaò cā.

tā gānjìng

Bǎoluó: *4th down, 15 to go. You're dead.*

Lìli: *You want to bet?*

Bǎoluó: *Yeah.*

Zhào XS: Lìli!

Lìli: *Hey, touchdown!*

Bǎoluó: *Beginner's luck.*   *dianzi yaoshe =*

Zhào XS: Lìli, Lìli, nǐ wènwen Bǎoluó, tā nèi yīfu shì shénmo liàozi de?

Lìli: Gànmo ya? Rénjiā zhèng máng zhe ne.

Zhào XS: Máng? Nǐ jiùshi máng wǎn(r). Hài, zhèi mábù dài, zhèi gēbozhǒu(r) hái bǔ gè bǔding.

burlapsack

tamen mángzhe wǎn(r).

Lìli: *Broken, there?*

Bǎoluó: *Oh, this? No. This is the style, this is fashion. This is the best, really. Pierre Cardin.*

Zhào XS: Zhèi kùzi yě shì qùnián de. Zhèi xiǎo huǒzi zhèng cuāngāo(r).

Lìli: Nǐ bié xiāshuō le. Rénjiā shì tiáo xīn kùzi, zuì shíxīng de yàngzi le.

Zhào XS: Dé-le-ba! Cūbù kùzi. Nǐ jiùjiu a, zài nèibiān(r) hùnde yě gòuqiàng, kùnnan a!

Bǎoluó: *No, you don't understand. These here, these are Calvin Kleins.*

Zhào XS: Zhèi shì wǒ zài wǔqī gànxiào láodòng shíhòu chuānde, yǒu hǎo jǐtiáo ne. Zhèi zài nèi Měiguó néng liúxíng ba?

Lìli: Bàba! *tan ji ta = play the guitar*

Dìjiǔjié

Dì Sìshíqī Mù--- Zài Zhàojiā wūli

Zhào TT: Āiyā, nǐ bié lǎo gēnzhe wǒ zhuànyou xíng bù-xíng a? Jìn àishì(r).

Zhào XS: À, wǒ shuō, zhèi Lìli jiù zhènmoge wǎn(r)fǎ, nǐ jiūjìng guǎn bù-guǎn?

Zhào TT: Nǐ gàn shénmo de? Nǐ gànmo bù-guǎn a?

danxin = to worry

31

Zhào XS: Zhèi, wǒ shuōdeshàng huà ma? Zhèige nǐmen mǔnǚ liǎng zhèige xīn-tiē-xīn de. Zìdǎ nǐ dìdi láile zhīhòua, jiù méi jiànguo tā niànguò yìtiān(r) shū.

Zhào TT: Hái zǎo ne.

zháoji = anxious, nervous, upset

huàiyingshan : bad influence

Zhào XS: Hái zǎo ne? Wǒ fān-le-fān rìlì, háiyǒu èrshísāntiān le. A, chéngtiān de gēn nèige bǎobèi Luó tīng xīyáng gēqǔ, yàobù, jiù dàizhe ěrjīzi bèngda. Wǒ kànzhe bièniu.

Zhào TT: Rénjiā jiào Bǎoluó, shì ge Měiguó háizi, tè huópo.

bu zunjing = respect ta baba

Zhào XS: Nǎguó háizi yě bù-chéng a, méishàng-méixià de. Tā nèitiān wǒ kàn tā qiāo tā bàba de nǎodai, nǐ nǎ(r) yǒu zhèi yàng de? A, zhēnde, chōukòng nín gēn nín bǎobèi gūniang tí-yi-tí.

méishàng-méixià = doesnt know where he belongs

Zhào TT: Pà shénmo ya, wànyī kǎo bù-jǔ, ràng xiǎodì gěi tā bàn Měiguó liúxué.

wo bù guan = I don't care....

Zhào XS: Nǐ shěde jiù zhènmo ge bǎobèi guǐnǚ a?

tài dù = attitude

Zhào TT: Hài, zǐnǚ dà le, jiù děi gè-bèn-qián-chéng, zài shuō, gēnzhe zìjǐ de qīn jiùjiu, zhèi yǒu shénmo bú-fàngxīn de.

xiao shang shuo hua = to whisper, speaking a small voice

Zhào XS: A, nǐ, nǐ dǒng shénmo, Měiguó de shèhuì a, bù-zhī yǒu duō luàn. Zhìān bù-hǎo, érqiě a, xìng guānxi tè luàn, háiyǒu mǎn jiē de tóng xìng liàn. Nòng bù-hǎo a, zài dài huílai ge yáng nǚxu.

Pengjing = bonzai tree   *zhìān = public order*

Dì Sìshíbā Mù--- Zài Běihǎi yèyútǐxiào

Dì Sìshíjiǔ Mù--- Zài Běijīng-Fàndiàn

hen jiliye de lianxi = to practice intensly

YángrénA: *How's your ping pong?*

lianxi = to practice
liuhan = to sweat

Bǎoluó: *My coach says I'm gonna be the best in the bunch, if I can just get my serve down. You know that singles title coming up? No problem, I'm gonna take it!*

huazhuang de hen
súqi = tacky

zikua = braggy

32

zhaoaou = cocky

danren jing dao san = single title

jiāo ào = arrogant, stuck up

Zai waimian de tangvar

YángrénB: *You're going to play against Liu? Lìli, didn't your boyfriend Liu win the title last year?*

YángrénA: *Alright, this is going to be hot! Is it a major match?*

Bǎoluó: *I don't know. It's major for me. Look at those two guys checking you out!*

YángrénB: *Look at this! They're really checking her out!*

YángrénA: *What's a nice girl like you doing hanging around with foreign devils like us?*

Dì Wǔshí Mù--- Zài Zhàojiā

Yáng guǐzi = foreign devil

Bǎoluó: *Mom, your favorite niece is in a funny mood. Again.*

taoxi = tease

Fāng TT: *Stop teasing her! Give her some privacy.*

Bǎoluó: *Oh, come on. I'm cool.*

Zhào TT: Ai, wǒ shuō a, jiào Lìli shōushi zhuōzi, mǎshàng chīfàn le.

Zhào XS: Hǎo lei.

zai yuanzi

Fāng TT: *Ready to move back to the hotel tonight?*

Lili yao xuexi

Bǎoluó: *Not really. I'm kinda getting used to this place. Developing my leg muscles.*

Zhào XS: Lìli, Lìli.

ràng Lìli fēnxīn = To distract Lìli

Lìli: Wǒ bù-chīfàn le.

Zhào XS:　　Wǒ shuō a, nǐ guǎnguan nǐ nǚr ba. Tā shuō zhùnbèi gāokǎo shíjiān láibùjí le.

Fāng TT:　　*We're moving back to the hotel. Your father told me this morning.*

Zhào XS:　　Cóng jīn(r) qǐ ₐjiù bù-chīfàn le.

lü dou = greenbeans

Bǎoluó:　　*Why? Just because of Lily?*

Zhào TT:　　Húshuō.

Fāng TT:　　*There is one thing in this country that causes more concern than the Super Bowl game back home. The annual college entrance examination.*

Bǎoluó:　　*I know, I know. It's like a one in a hundred chance, and if you don't make it then you have to sell tea in the streets. Well, I think Lily'd make a beautiful tea peddler.*

Fāng TT:　　*Go inside and pack!!*

da shou mao = teddy bear

Dìshíjié

Dì Wǔshíyī Mù--- Zài Lìli de wòfáng

Zhào TT:　Lìli, Lìli, chūlái chīfàn!

ta xianzai è bu

rang ziji faofeng = drive oneself insane

Lìli:　　Aīyā, mā, wǒ gēn nǐ shuōguò le, gāokǎo zhīqián wǒ bù-chū fángmén.

è bu = intensively cram

Zhào TT:　À! Zhèi wūzi zěnmo zāng chéng zhèi yàng? Zhè nóngmàoshìchǎng shìde. Lái! Kuài! Kuàibǎ zhèi wǎn zhūgān tāng hē le.

farmers free market

Lìli:　　Wǒ bù-hē.

zhūgān tāng:

gān yán = hepatitis

Zhào TT: Kuài! Bú-è yě jiē guò qu. Kuài! Tàngzhe nǐ mā de shǒu le. Kuài diǎn(r)! Aīyo!

Lìli: Nǐ shuō, wǒ gāokǎo zhīqián bèi zìdiǎn, hái láidejí ma?

Zhào TT: À, xiān bǎ zhèiwǎn zhūgān tāng hē le, a. Chèn rè hē le. Zhèi bù-chīfàn nǎr xíng a!
"Rén-shi-tiě, fàn-shi-gāng", yídùn bù-chī tā bú è de huāng.

hen bú = nutrians

Dì Wǔshíèr Mù--- Gāokǎo qiánxī zài Liújiā

Liú XS: Shénmo shíhòu le, shuì ba!

Yida
zhunbei kaoshi

Yīdá: Zài dāi yìhuǐ(r).

Dì Wǔshísān Mù---Gāokǎo qiánxī zài Zàojiā

Zhào TT: Zhūgāntāng hē le bú-shàng liǎng kǒu.

Zhào XS: Nǐ nèi zhūgāntāng a, zhēn bù-zěnmo hǎo hē.

Zhào TT: Zhèi jǐtiān tā zhēnde lián fángmén dōu bù-chū, cèsuǒ dōu méi-shàng, zěnmo déliǎo
a!

wang shang kan =
to look down

Zhào XS: Bù-chī bù-hē, yě jiù bù-lā-bù-sā.

dǐ tóu = head down

Dì Wǔshísì Mù--- Zài Lìli de wòfáng

jiaolian = coach   *Tamen yong taijia zuo lili*

taijia = stretcher

Lìli: ...māma! Māma!

jinguchē = ambulence

Yida qu kaoshi

zhào xs qu qasu zhao tt

35

lili shi hun dao le.

Zhào TT: Wǒ shuō, ...

Dì Wǔshíwǔ Mù--- Zài kǎochǎng
Dì Wǔshíliù Mù--- Zài Liújiā

Zăihuá: Liǎngdiǎn duō le éi, qǐ bu-qǐ? Méi-qì(r), meí-qì(r).

Yīdá: Shǒu wàng nǎr ge guò le, xié chòu, xié chòu de.

Zăihuá: Méi wéi(r) a! Chūqù guàngguang. Lǎo dāi zài jiā gànmo a? Huódòng, huódòng.

Yīdá: Gàn shénmo? Gāokǎo yě guòle, zài kǎo hái děi děng dào míngnián ne.

Zăihuá: Tīngting zhèige.

Línjū: Bié chàng le. Xiàde Sān Gēr niào kàng le.

Zăihuá: Lìli chū yuàn le. Nǎtiān zán kànkan tā qù. Rénjiā xiànzài gēn zánmen yíyàng yě shì dàiyè qīngnián le. Jiàoliàn ràng nǐ liàn qiú qù na.

Yīdá: Dà rè tiān, liàn shénmo qiú a?

Zăihuá: Jiù yào bǐsài le.

Yīdá: *So what?* na zenmeyang?

Zăihuá: Jiàoliàn shuō le, nǐ yào bù-hǎohāo liàn xí, cānjiā bǐsài, guànjūn fēi jiào Fāng Bǎoluó nèi bǎobèi luó(r) gěi duān le.

Dì Wǔshíqī Mù--- Zài Běihǎi yèyútǐxiào

36

Jiàoliàn: Nǐ zhèi qiú dǎ de bú-cuò, zùijìn nǐ tíng yǒu jìnbù de. Hǎohāo liàn.

Bǎoluó: Xièxie.

díren = rival, enenmy

yíh = winner

da bu dao = to miss a shot

hen duan de duan kuzi = short shorts

zai tǐyùguan = gym

Dì Wǔshíbā Mù--- Sàiqiú

competition

"qingnian = youth union - on his shirt

Bàogào yuán: Fāng Bǎoluó shì Měiguó Jiāzhōu qū shàoniánzǔ pīngpāng guànjūn. Lìng
        yíweì juésài xuǎnshǒu shì Liú Yīdá.   *biao fenshude = scoreboard*

henji lie = intense

Yida gen ta woshuo = shake hands

shi liu bi ershi yi fen = scoreboard

youren zhichi = crowd support

fen = point

du fen = to score

pīng fen = tied score

kàn guanzhong = crowd

caipàn = referee

fànqur = break rule

mandangzuo = slow motion

ping pong tai = ping pong table

peng taizi = hit table

Dì Wǔshíjiǔ Mù--- Zài Tǐyùguǎn gēnyīshǐ

zhuozi = table

Buoyinyuan = announcers

Zǎihuá: Gērmen(r), nǐ gàile!   *Yida jia you: bǐo Yida*

Fāng XS: *How do you feel dick breath?*

gēnyīshǐ = locker room

Bǎoluó: *Oh, great. Just great.*   *da lai dagu = play back + forth*

er shi yi bi jiu = 21 to 9

Fāng XS: *You had a tough match tonight, Didn't you?*

shéngqi = angry

Bǎoluó: *I play to win. I hate losing. I hate it so much.*

shīwàng = disappointed

Fāng XS: *Listen, son, you see...you played the best game ever. Well, you didn't win the
        championship. You gave the best performance, the best shots, and that's a
        victory by itself. Can you understand that? You see, in each tournament there's
        only one champ, but many winners. I think today you are one of them, winners...*

37

Bǎoluó: Dad, I'm kinda hungry, you know. So, why don't you save your bullshit.

Fāng XS: Okay, why don't you let me treat you to one of those grand Peking duck feast with a warm Coca-Cola?

Bǎoluó: Okay. You know, if you wanna say it right, you gotta say penis breath...

Dì Liùshí Mù--- Zài Liújiā ménqián qìngzhù Yīdá kǎoshàng dàxué

Dì Liùshíyī Mù--- Zài Fāngjiā

Wilson: Hi Grace!

Fāng TT :   Mr. Wilson, what a surprise.

Wilson: My, you look lovely.

Fāng TT: Thank you, it's a Chinese peasant blouse.

Wilson: Elegant.

Fāng TT: Do come in.

Wilson: How was your trip to China?

Fāng TT: Oh, it was wonderful.

Bǎoluó: People in America think I'm too Chinese, and then people in China think I'm too American. What do you think about that? "   Bossman!"

Linda: Meiyoo, meiyo. Hey, bossman.

Bǎoluó: No, you have to say "méiyǒu". Wǒmen zhèr méiyǒu.

Fāng TT: The Chinese doctors stuck needles in his back. It gave him a funny tingling sensation, but it worked. Worked like a charm.

Wilson: Magic, magic. Looking good, Leo!

(Jù Zhōng)

honorable
guangrong kaoshang beijing daxue

jingzhu = celebrate
gongxi = contratulations

da gu = to drum